God's

Radical

Remnant

God's Radical Remnant

Taking Jesus to the World

by Bill Henderson

Published by
Henderson International Ministries, Inc.

Cover Design by Ben Nichols
Editing/Proofreading/Formatting by Marty Shull

Scripture quotations in this publication are taken from

Printed by 3Cross Publishing 2005
9757 Widmer Road, Lenexa KS 66215
Toll Free 877.626.7596
www.3CrossPublishing.com

Dedication

This book is lovingly dedicated to my Lord and Savior, Jesus Christ and to my family members who are in the grandstands of heaven, among the great cloud of witnesses. I will forever cherish the memory of their lives and press toward eternity to see them.

My father William
My mother Carolyn
My daughter Jessica Lynn
My nephew Timothy

*To yesterday's companions
and tomorrow's reunion!*

Acknowledgements

To my lovely wife, Mary Ann, God's helpmate and my best friend—I love you more than words can say. Thanks for your hard work. You have your ducks in a row!

To Victoria Peluso, my mother-in-law, intercessor, and dear friend. I cannot begin to tell you how your prayers have carried me many times. You are a true woman of God.

To my precious sister, Carolyn Copeland, for her wisdom, counsel and tasty meals between chapters.

To her husband, Bob, for his many years of prayer and patience.

Special thanks to

~My pastor Dutch Sheets for helping me recognize the importance of this book.

~Jonathan Gainsbrugh and Apostle Jonas Clark for their many hours of labor. You two made me look good!

~ Pastors Matt and Amy Stoehr for their encouragement when I needed it the most.

~Marty Shull, my editor and incredible woman of patience, grace and skill!

~Ben Nichols for his awesome and speedy cover design.

~Susan Strong who answered our 911 cover call.

~Pastor Kurt Routon, Church of God in Victoria, Texas.

~Lulu Auger for her great faith in this endeavor. You are family and we love you!

~Mona Kraeer for her friendship and belief in this book.

Steve and Judy Holm, Joey Knight, Steve Wamberg, Bob and Edith Ecker, Jim and Charlene Nelson, and those precious saints of God who gather every Thursday evening in our home for a study in the Word.

To all of those who have helped to make this book a reality. Without your love, support and prayers, this would not have been possible. There are too many to list!

And last but not least, to all of those who desire to become radical and passionate in your love and service for Jesus and whose aim it is to hear him say, "Well done, good and faithful servant."

Let the reformation begin!

Table of Contents

Foreword

God's Radical Remnant—what a book! I totally enjoyed reading it and believe that it will minister life to you. You know, the Bible is full of radicals. Jesus was the greatest radical of them all. Moses was a radical, so was the Apostle Paul and St. Peter—the list of radicals in the Word goes on and on. I believe that it has always taken radical men and women to bring about change in this world and today is no different. God is still looking for people of faith who will not be afraid to follow Him and be radical fishers of men, whatever the cost.

I thank Bill for writing a book like this because so many people today need to know that there is a radical within every believer. In *God's Radical Remnant*, Bill will open your eyes to the pure joy and power of radical, grassroots evangelism. The true stories he shares aren't just entertaining, they are inspirational! They will inspire you to break free from whatever has been holding you back from being bold for God and find your own "inner radical!" That boldness of the Holy Ghost is in you and now, it's time to let Him out!

I certainly enjoyed this book and I know you will too. So, sit down with a good cup of coffee and read this glorious book. I believe you'll learn some things about God that you didn't know existed. You'll also learn some things about yourself that you didn't know existed! You'll enjoy it!

Bill, thanks for putting out a book that cuts right to the chase when it comes to telling others about Jesus. Your book lets us all know that Jesus was indeed a radical. And if Jesus was a radical, then we all ought to be radicals, too! I loved it!

God bless you as you read Bill's inspiring book, *God's Radical Remnant*!

Dr. Jesse Duplantis
International Evangelist and Author

Foreword

Bill Henderson is a New Testament evangelist who has seemingly "walked off the pages of the Bible" into the 21st century. His boldness in witness and everyday life makes a strong impact in the lives of many people. Acts 1:8 (KJV) quotes Jesus as saying that "you shall receive power after the Holy Spirit comes upon you and you shall be witnesses unto me" in your hometown (Jerusalem), in the surrounding region (Judea), in the impenetrable areas where you are not welcome and which you consider to be on the wrong side of the tracks (Samaria), "and unto the uttermost parts of the earth."

Bill has truly been a powerful voice and fearless proclaimer of the Gospel in all of those places mentioned in Acts 1:8. I met Bill Henderson on the streets of Jamaica. God had previously radically saved me and called me into the ministry of Jesus Christ. After starting a church in my hometown and ministering there as a Pastor, one day the Lord spoke to my heart that He was additionally calling me to be a "street preacher." I was to go to Jamaica and preach on the streets. When I met Bill in Jamaica, God joined two radicals at heart who would do whatever and go wherever Jesus said.

Since that fateful encounter, Bill and I have preached together for over 20 years in open air and street meetings, as well as in *Glorious Holy Ghost Church Services*. When we get together, it seems that God notches up the intensity.

Bill has many stories to tell... stories about the saving and delivering power of Jesus Christ in our generation. Stories about how God can take a former drug addict and street fighter, then use him to face down the devil, release God's anointing to tear down strongholds, and bring freedom to those who were tormented in bondage and captivity.

I pray that these accounts of ministry exploits challenge the church to take the Gospel to the streets and to people who are in their own circle of influence. I pray that individuals who read this book will make the decision to enlist as part of Jesus' radical remnant on the earth today and to embark on their own exploits of faith.

In Christ's Service,
Dr. Jules Boquet
Harvest Cathedral Ministries
Houma, Louisiana

Foreword

Perhaps more than any other time in history, the words of Jesus regarding the fields being overripe for harvest speak to the times and seasons of the 21st century Christian community. Interestingly enough, those words were spoken by Jesus to His disciples immediately following a powerful encounter Jesus had with the woman of Samaria who met Him outside of town, after hours, when it was safe for her to draw water. She had some unfinished business in her past that made her an object of scorn in her community.

Jesus spoke to her in a casual conversation and then began to operate in the word of knowledge and the word of wisdom to speak to her deepest need for intimacy and connectivity. In actual fact, this is the first record in all of the gospel accounts of what my dear friend Bill Henderson refers to as "prophetic evangelism."

If ever we needed to reach the lost, the bruised, the broken, and the disenfranchised with something more substantial than a few religious catch phrases, we need it now. We need an army of bold and faithful warriors who worship the Father in spirit and truth, and out of intimacy with Him, can be entrusted with the secrets of the hearts of those who are in our harvest fields. There are multitudes in the valley of decision, and in a day when so many people are seeking answers, there is a need for the recovery of the power of intimacy and revelation in speaking to the needs of the masses.

I urge you, take this book that you hold in your hand, pour over the pages in prayer and faith, and apply the spiritual life-lessons and life strategies regarding prophetic evangelism from one of the leading prophetic evangelists in the Body of Christ.

Thanks, Bill, for sharing the secrets of the Lord regarding the supernatural and its essential place in evangelism that the Lord has shared with you. We are indebted to your pioneering spirit and your mentoring mantle.

Dr. Mark J. Chironna
Mark Chironna Ministries
Orlando, Florida

Introduction
by the author, Bill Henderson

Many times, the word remnant describes someone who has survived many slaughters and one who has died to pride. They press through until they get a breakthrough.

Within the pages of this book are nearly thirty years of real and personal radical remnant experiences that I call radical evangelism. The purpose of these testimonies is to bring to you, the reader, not just inspiration and motivation, but also a spirit of impartation. What God has done for others, he will do for you, too.

Jesus said, "Follow me and I will make you fishers of men" (Matthew 4:19). The word make is the Greek word *payeao*, meaning that God will ordain you, band together with you, direct you, cause you to use your gifts, skills, talents, artistic abilities and help you win souls repeatedly.

Different kinds of fish require different kinds and sizes of hooks. All people are unique and different, so what may work for one might not necessarily work for another. God confirms His Word by His Spirit and He will use our different personalities and giftings to win souls.

The Word says, "They *overcame* him by the blood of the Lamb and the word of their testimony and they did not love their lives, even unto the death" (Revelation 12:11, italics added). The word overcame in the Greek language is *nikeo*, meaning to ....

> overwhelm,
> subdue,
> conquer,
> prevail,
> get the victory.

> "...the kingdom of heaven suffereth violence, and the violent take it by force."
> (Matthew 11:12b KJV)

The word testimony literally means evidence, record, report or witness. Our personal testimony, coupled with the Word of God, is the most powerful thing that we possess even if death threatens us.

> "Now therefore go and I will be with your mouth and teach you what to say."
> (Exodus 4:12 NKJV)

He didn't say, "NO." He said, "GO!" God is raising up a generation of apostolic soul-winners. In Matthew 4:4 it is written, "Man shall not live by bread alone, but by every word that proceeds from the mouth of God." The word proceeds in Greek is *ekporevonal*. It means currently coming forth. The Lord will use anyone who will answer the call of the Great Commission.

> "And he said unto them, Go ye into all the world and preach the gospel to every creature." (Mark 16:15 KJV)

CHAPTER 1

TRACT BOUQUET

"But God hath chosen the foolish
things of the world to confound the
wise; and God hath chosen the weak
things of the world to confound the
things which are mighty."
(I Corinthians 1:27 KJV)

Helen Shellnut's Homecoming

Helen, one of my mother's best Christian
friends, had passed away. Her daughter
contacted me and said, "Bill, we want you to
do Mom's funeral." I'd never done a funeral
before. I'd been a Christian for only a short
time. The only thing I knew to do then (and
still know to do now) when I don't know how
or what to do, is to pray. Prayer is never
wrong. That's why God's Word doesn't sug-
gest prayer, but commands us in I Thessa-
lonians 5:17: "Pray without ceasing."

As far as I knew, this wonderful Christian
lady Helen had a son that was a Satan wor-
shiper. I had run into him a couple of times.
At these previous encounters, he wanted to
smack me several different times but he
claimed that he couldn't because something
invisible had held back his hand.

During the days before the funeral, I got in
the shower and prayed. Then I prayed again

and still I prayed some more. As God is my witness, I was in that shower for four hours. After a short time, the shower went cold but that didn't stop me. I adapted and endured the freezing cold water while sitting down in the shower and praying in the Spirit.

Gospel Tracts

During this extended time of prayer in that cold shower, I had a vision. I saw myself placing a handful of gospel tracts into Helen's hands in the casket—like a bouquet of flowers. Then I said silently to myself, "This is awesome! This is the way I need to do it at the funeral."

I shared this "revelation" with someone who got very nervous and asked me, "Did you test the spirits?" I said a strong, "Yes! Of course." I didn't want to miss God, so I prayed, "Lord, if you don't want me to place those tracts in Helen's hands, then I won't. Just let me know for sure and I'll gladly go another way."

The Big Day Arrives

So the day of my first funeral arrived. To be perfectly honest, I was very nervous. You probably would be too. I had known this wonderful lady since I was 13 years old. Now I was 28 and she had been my mom's best friend. Helen had lived across the street from us and had invited us to church many times.

Before my mother died, she and Helen talked about the Lord all the time. You could always hear them talking about Jesus. It was, "Jesus, Jesus, Jesus!" So here I was doing my first funeral, wanting to honor both my mom and this wonderful Christian lady, Helen.

At the funeral parlor, I went up front at the appropriate time. I started the ceremony but immediately found myself not knowing what to say or do. I was thoroughly perplexed. About the third sentence into the message, I began telling people, "I've known this lady really well since I was 13 years old." However, instead of calling her Helen, I mistakenly started calling her Shellen.

Helen's full name was Helen Shellnut. But during the funeral service, I was nervous and called her Shellen Hellnut. I know the Spirit of God prays for me, making intercessions and requests that can't be put into articulate speech (Romans 8:26).

"Shellen was such a nice lady. Shellen was my mom's best friend and Shellen Hellnut was the type of lady who welcomed you to her house any time. She would feed you and really care for you."

I remember looking at the crowd and thinking, "I must really be making a monkey's uncle out of myself because their eyebrows are frequently raising and they are looking at me with strange faces." They were probably thinking, "Shellen Hellnut? You mean Helen Shellnut! Just how close were you?"

Everyone at the funeral parlor was dressed in black and taking things very seriously. My spirit wanted Jesus to do something really spectacular at this funeral. After all, Jesus never attended a funeral and left death as the victor. I only wanted what the Lord Himself wanted. I just didn't want to wimp out if the Lord would have me do something different, something daring, something unusual in Helen's home-going funeral service. In my mind, I had this debate going on. My mind was saying, "Maybe I should back off and just do a normal funeral." It seems that Satan is always throwing doubt at us and trying to keep us from obeying God's voice.

Fortunately that morning, I had already stuffed my suit jacket pocket full of tracts. They had printed on the front, in great big letters, *The Big Question.* I had done that just in case the funeral service actually went in that direction. All of a sudden I felt the Lord say to me, "Put those tracts in Helen's hands in the casket up front, just like I showed you."

Wanting to obey God's leading, I pulled out a fistful of gospel tracts, walked over to the casket and began to place them in her hands. Then looking at the crowd, I said, "Ladies and gentlemen, if Shellen could sit up in this

coffin right now, Shellen herself would personally hand you one of these tracts because
she wants you to be where she is now.
Shellen is with Jesus. Right now, even as you
sit here, Shellen is in heaven to be eternally
with Jesus Christ her Lord and Savior!"

Reach Out and Touch Someone

Then I said, "She's just a shell of a woman.
So don't be a nut. Don't be a fool. Be cool and
make heaven." I continued, "When you walk
by Helen's casket today, don't just stare.
Don't just gawk. Don't look at the empty shell
of a woman. Don't be nuts. Just reach in and
allow Shellen (here we go again) to hand you
a gospel tract. Don't just let her hand it to
you. I want you to read it." I pressed on: "So
now everybody, I want you to stand to your
feet right now. Please form a single-file line
and come to the front and allow Shellen to
hand you a tract." I thought, "Oh well, I'm in
this by myself now. What should I do?"

One by one, everybody walked up front by
the casket where I was standing. Some of the
people smiled, reached in and took the gospel
tract with joy. You could obviously tell that
these were Christians. In contrast, some of
the funeral attendees were not. As they
walked by the casket, some had a look of
horror on their faces. Some wouldn't even
look at Helen or me. Others looked at me as if
to say, "What ARE you doing?!" Some would
blindly reach their hand toward the gospel

tracts and miss because they didn't want to look directly at Helen in the casket or at the gospel tract either. With some of the more reluctant ones, I just grabbed their wrists and guided their shaking hands toward the tract.

When everybody was done filing by, I specifically remember Helen's son. He was the last one in line. He walked by but refused to put his hand forward to take a tract. He just stood there and literally squared off with me as if he wanted to fight. Then he began to shake and turn red. I just reached over and gently patted him on the shoulder and said, "Everything's going to be okay." He was vibrating with rage and was just barely keeping it under control.

He told me five years later that he had his fist clenched in his pocket as he was thinking, "I am going to break this crazy preacher's nose right here in front of God and everybody at this funeral!" He also told me that he had felt something grab his wrist and hold it down in his pocket. He went back to his seat without taking a tract. I know that was either the Lord or one of my angels protecting me at that funeral, as it says in Psalms 91:11, "He shall give His angels charge over you, to keep you in all your ways."

The Big Question

Now it was time to go to the gravesite. Once assembled there, I asked the crowd, "How many people received a tract from Helen? Well, Helen and Jesus want me to go through this tract with you right now." I just read the tract out loud. Remember it was called *The Big Question*. It had steps one, two, three and four to salvation. We went through it together as I read all the steps out loud. At the end of that short gospel tract was a salvation prayer.

Then I said, "Now folks, Helen herself has prayed that same prayer that is in this gospel tract. I'm going to pray that same prayer right now. Everyone who wants to go where Helen is, everyone who does not want to go to hell, but instead who wants to go to heaven, I want you to put your hands up in the air before we pray this prayer." Silently praying in my heart, I was begging Jesus for just one soul, "Please Lord let there be at least one hand." To my utter surprise and amazement, between 40 and 50 hands went up into the air. One fellow sitting in a wheelchair shot both hands up into the air!

Then, out loud, we went through the sinner's salvation prayer together. I led them in the prayer as they repeated the sentences after me. The prayer was something like this:

Lord, I thank you that you have extended your great love to us and all mankind. Lord, I thank you that you have extended your great love to us, that while we were sinners and separated from you, you sent your Son, Jesus Christ, to pay the price for our sins by dying on the cross. Lord, I thank you for the blood sacrifice that Jesus made by giving His own life in my place so that I could, by that sacrifice, be made righteous in your sight. Lord Jesus, I ask you to come into my heart. To forgive my sins. To wash me with your sinless blood and to become my Lord and Savior, both now and forever."

After we prayed that prayer, I asked that graveside congregation to come forward as we lowered Helen into the ground. We would all see her again one day.

Helen's daughter who had asked me to do the funeral was so happy. Afterwards, she came to me and thanked me numerous times. She said, "Bill, I want you to know that my entire family gave their hearts to Jesus today except my one brother." That was one of the most awesome days of my life.

Summary

"Now therefore go, and I will be with thy mouth, and teach thee what thou shalt say." (Exodus 4:12 KJV)

It is easy to look back and see the Holy
Spirit leading me at that funeral. But before
God justified what He told me to do, it re-
quired both faith and obedience on my part. I
had to act in faith before seeing the manifes-
tation of His plan, regardless of how it looked
to others or what others thought.

To put a bouquet of tracts into the hands of
the deceased is something that you may
never do. I may never do it again either. But
as already mentioned, Jesus never attended a
funeral and left death as the victor. He is still
the same, "Yesterday, today, and forever"
(Hebrews 13:8).

Step out in faith and obedience to the
prompting of the Holy Spirit. He will back you
up every time and bless you as you fulfill the
Great Commission.

> "O Death, I will be your plague; O
> Grave, I will be your destruction."
> (Hosea 13:14 NKJV)

> "But God hath chosen the foolish
> things of the world to confound the
> wise; and God hath chosen the weak
> things of the world to confound the
> things which are mighty."
> (1 Corinthians 1:27)

The Word of God tells us, "...he that
winneth souls is wise" (Proverbs 11:30). The

Hebrew word for wise is *chakam*, meaning wise, strategic, cunning, crafty, intelligent, skillful, artful, subtle, learned and shrewd.

Choose one or more of these 10 meanings for the word *wise* that you think ties into this testimony.

[ ] wise   [ ] strategic
[ ] cunning   [ ] crafty
[ ] intelligent   [ ] skillful
[ ] artful   [ ] subtle
[ ] learned   [ ] shrewd

Validations

If you are ready for an extraordinary, life-inspiring book on being always ready to share your faith and snatch others from hell, then you are in for a treat! I wondered how Bill would select the stories for this book since he has hundreds of them. I always knew that his rambunctious energy, once used to serve self and the enemy, would be just as outrageous for the Kingdom of God, once he yielded his heart to the Lord.

I personally attended the funeral Helen Shellnut and witnessed the gospel tracts placed in her hands. Knowing that God is the author who created all personalities, He desires to work through our uniqueness to reach a lost and dying world as we are willing. Bill has done just that since the night he called me in December of 1978 saying, "I've REALLY found Jesus!"

In all the years since, through much joy and tribulation, Bill has never walked away from this passion and sense of urgency in his soul.

I am honored to be able to say that Bill Henderson is my brother, friend and the MOST radical, consistent soul-winner I've ever known! He truly is focused on eternity and God can call on Bill 24/7 and he always answers.

Carolyn Copeland
Bill's sister

~~~

I was indeed at the funeral of Helen Shellnut, and sang for the service and at graveside. In the Spirit of Peter, Bill, always brash and bold for the Lord, placed tracts in Helen's hand, and invited folks to take one.

Paul said in I Corinthians 4:9b, "We are made a spectacle unto the world, and to angels, and to men. We are fools for Christ's sake..."

Gwen Mills
Bill's Spiritual Mother

CHAPTER 2

SLEDGEHAMMER

"Is not my word like as a fire? saith the Lord; like a hammer that breaketh the rock in pieces?" (Jeremiah 23:29 KJV)

Cadence Calls

We were in a city called Porterville, California, where we had entered a parade. Our evangelism ministry team had about thirty or so people.

The parade organizers didn't know that we were Christians. We were all dressed up in army khakis and red shirts with Christian slogans. We had turned our hats and shirts inside out so that you couldn't see exactly what they said. We didn't want them to see our "colors." Some of our shirts had a picture of the devil with a circle around it and a line through it. The parade organizers asked us, "What do you do?" We told them that we were soldiers and that we did cadence calls. They allowed us to enter the parade.

Before we entered the parade, I had spent some time praying in the Spirit. While in prayer, I saw myself preaching to a large crowd of people but I didn't know how it was going to take place. I prayed, "Lord, how is this supposed to happen?" I was thinking maybe it was going to happen by preaching in a church but we were not even booked to preach in a church. We were just in the city helping others win souls. So when we entered the parade, I thought maybe that was my opportunity because I saw the cameras rolling and knew that multitudes would be watching. Maybe that's what the Lord was showing me in prayer.

Our time came and cadence calls were exactly what we did. We had waited strategically for that perfect and exact point in the parade route. I had a Sergeant Carter hat—you know, like Gomer Pyle. Anyway, as we got going, marching in the parade, the main cadence that we all repeated went like this...

"I don't know what you've been told,

Jesus Christ will save your soul.

He died for you, He died for me.

And now He wants to set you free.

Booze and drugs are not the way,

Cause Jesus said, 'I am the Way.'

J – E – S – U – S!"

You should have been there. As we rounded the corner, we shouted this cadence many times. You should have seen their faces.

Wow! Everybody, especially the judges, everyone there, their mouths were just hanging
open, just staring at us with stunned faces
and probably thinking, "What is this?" Wow,
we had a great time!

Setup Guy

Afterwards, we were going to the fairgrounds and park because there were all
types of booths and games such as bobbing
for apples and pin the tail on the donkey.

Somebody said, "Hey Bill, do you see that
car over there? You can give the guy a dollar
and then you can hit that old car with a
sledgehammer." He continued, "I can just see
you over there pounding that car with the
sledgehammer and then preaching to the
people."

Just as John the Baptist was the "setup
guy" for Jesus, quite a number of times,
different people have been the "setup guy" for
me. I answered, "Hey, you got the idea, so
why don't *you* go over and do it?"

God's setup guy responded and said, "No,
man, it's you. It fits you!"

I said, "Well, we'll see." I walked toward the
demolition car praying, "Lord, if you really
want me to do this, confirm it somehow. Have
the guy say something to me."

Now, please visualize this. The guy running the sledgehammer event was a Danny DeVito look-alike. He was a little short, fat guy with a big cigar. He looked like he came from Chicago. From across the way, he looked at me and said, "Hey you with the beard and the blonde hair and the muscled arms. Yeah, you! Hey, come on over here."

You could see that the demolition car had been beat up some but there had not been too many people doing it. This guy was standing there with a sledgehammer, trying to get somebody to beat up his car, but nobody was coming forward to try their hand at it.

So I prayed, "Okay, Lord, let's just test the waters a little bit." I said to the guy running the sledgehammer game, "Hey, I'll make you a deal."

He replied, "Just give me some money and you got a deal."

I told him, "You let me get on top of that car and I'll do it."

He responded with that "Southside Chicagee" accent, "You give me a couple of bucks and you can get UNDER the car, you can get IN the car, or you can get ON TOP OF the car. Money talks or the sledgehammer walks. Okay?"

Somebody handed him a $5 bill. I learned years later it was one of my brothers, Ronnie. He was standing there shouting, "Go for it! Go for it!" I knew I had a couple of swats in me.

Frozen

So I climbed up on top of the car and was standing there, holding the sledgehammer. I was thinking in my heart and praying, "Oh Lord!" Many people were looking at me and laughing.

Then I heard the Lord say to me in my spirit, "I want you to worship me." I set the sledgehammer between my legs, raised my hands in the air and just froze. Now I was standing on top of an old car with my hands in the air.

All the time I was praying, "Where are You Lord? Why are You doing this to me?"

I said to myself, "Okay, I'm not even gonna peek. I'm just gonna worship You, Jesus. I'm gonna praise You." I was standing there like a department store mannequin.

When I first climbed on top of that car there were a few people watching, but after a few minutes I peeked and to my amazement, there were close to 100 people standing there looking at me—this guy standing on top of the car. After I peeked and saw the crowd, I prayed, "Oh my God, I can't believe it! Jesus, now I see what you're doing!" So I grabbed the sledgehammer and prayed, "Lord, give me the words."

Suddenly I felt as if there was fire in my eyes. I wasn't nervous any more. I had peace and an anointing of divine tenacity. It seemed I was making direct eye contact with each person there. They were all staring at me and I was looking back at them. I raised my voice to the top of my lungs and yelled as loud as I could, "Two thousand years ago there was war in heaven...," and I went CRASH with the sledgehammer. Then the whole park came running over to see what was going on. Everywhere people stopped whatever they were doing. Children that had been running stopped. Everybody stopped and looked at me on top of that car. Somebody told me there were at least several hundred people who were drawn to that car.

I continued to preach with my mighty sledgehammer in my hand, "God and the devil had a fight. But God is stronger than the devil and God kicked the devil out of heaven like lightning ." The people heard another CRASH as I pounded that car with the sledgehammer. I was in an anointed flow and a rhythm between preaching the Word of God and slamming that car with the sledgehammer.

CRASH! I continued preaching. CRASH! I preached some more. The crowd continued to get bigger and bigger. Many in the crowd were cheering me on, "Yea! Yea!" The group from the parade was cheering me on. Their shouts of encouragement really provided an exciting atmosphere for the crowd. "You go for it!"

CRASH! Preach! CRASH! Preach! Yea!

Stuck Forever

All of a sudden, with a mighty CRASH, the sledgehammer went through the roof of the car and was stuck. I was jerking and jerking, but I couldn't pull it out. I was praying, "Oh God, what now? What am I gonna do, Lord?" Many in the crowd were starting to giggle. I was jerking and jerking but couldn't get that sledgehammer out of that car. It was stuck.

Then I said, "Ladies and gentlemen," as I was pulling with all of my strength, "just like this sledgehammer is stuck, if you ever go to hell, you will be stuck forever." The crowd erupted. It was almost like applause. You could hear screams of "yeaaaah!" The Christians in the crowd were applauding and happy. Those who weren't saved were just clapping their hands sort of mechanically.

Finally, I just pulled on that sledgehammer with all my might and a loud groan and out it came. Because the handle had been previously cracked, it had been duct-taped together. You could see it was broken, but dangling and held together by the duct tape. So there I was, out of breath, sweating profusely, standing on top of the car, and holding up a broken sledgehammer in my hand.

Break the Devil's Neck

Looking at the people from the top of the car, I said, "Ladies and gentlemen, in case you're wondering, I'm a preacher and I am acting out my sermon. What I said is very, very real. Just like the neck of this sledgehammer is broken, the day you ask Jesus to come into your life and come into your heart, this is what you do to the devil. You break the devil's neck!"

Then I said, "I gave my life to the Lord several years ago after a drug overdose. How many people here have enough guts to raise your hand and say, 'I want that same Jesus! I want to serve Jesus too!'" Again to my shock and surprise, just like at Helen Shellnut's funeral, numerous hands went up everywhere!

Then I said to our parade group, "Reach over and grab a hand and let's all pray together right now." I led them all, right then and there, in a salvation prayer. Because the soul-winning team was strategically scattered throughout the crowd, we were able to counsel and personally talk with each person that prayed the sinner's prayer with me.

I climbed down from the car and the guy with the cigar had a shocked look on his face that declared, "I never seen anything like this in my life!" In his hand was a fist full of money as people were giving him money to keep me pounding and preaching.

Gang Fight Stopped

Now, here's the cherry-on-the-cake of this story. Afterwards, I was walking around the fairgrounds when all of a sudden this one guy drags another guy over to me and says, "Hey! How are you doing?"

I shook his hand and asked, "So, were you one of those afraid to raise their hand over there?"

He responded, "No! I prayed way over there the prayer you told all the people to pray with you."

I looked to where he was pointing. In the distance there was a shed about a half football field away, maybe 50 to 60 yards. I asked, "You could hear me all the way over there?"

He replied, "Man, you are one very loud preacher man!"

I said, "That's cool. So tell me, did you mean the prayer you said you prayed?"

He looked down and his eyes were teary. This other fellow that was with him seemed to be a youth pastor. He added, "Bill, this is so and so. There are two gangs in this town and this guy is the leader of one of the gangs."

He continued, "Bill, you don't know this, but while you were up there preaching on top of the car and beating it up with the sledgehammer, these two gang leaders were way over there, battling it out with broken bottles because they had vowed to kill each other. They had been circling one another, taking swipes at each other's throats with these broken bottles in their hands. But praise God, somehow they both heard you preaching and eventually it caused them to stop and listen. Bill, this guy here ended up giving his life to the Lord."

I was rejoicing in my heart. Then I asked the newly saved gang leader, "Hey, tell me, where's the rest of your gang?" He pointed to a group of guys in the distance. We both walked slowly to them and talked to them. A few more of them prayed with us and gave their lives to the Lord. Scripture declares, "And from the days of John the Baptist until now, the kingdom of heaven suffereth violence, and the violent take it by force" (Matthew 11:12 KJV).

God provides every believer with a violent faith to break through. Violent faith is extremely energetic, passionate, zealous and enforces the Word of God.

Summary

A soul winner is an opportunist. He follows the leading of the Holy Spirit as God sets up various events and opportunities to share the gospel. Seizing the moment is vitally important in advancing the gospel of Jesus Christ. God may not call upon everyone to jump on top of a car at a fair, but every believer can step out in faith. This testimony proves God's faithfulness to watch over His Word to perform it. So we learn the following principles.

PRAYER IN THE SPIRIT
> "For he that speaketh in an unknown tongue speaketh not unto men, but unto God: for no man understandeth him; howbeit in the spirit he speaketh mysteries."
> (I Corinthians 14:2 KJV)

WISDOM TO OVERCOME OPPOSITION
> "If any of you lack wisdom, let him ask of God, that giveth to all men liberally, and upbraideth not; and it shall be given him." (James 1:5 KJV)

GOD CONFIRMS HIS WORD
WITH SIGNS FOLLOWING

"And they went forth, and preached everywhere, the Lord working with them, and confirming the word with signs following. Amen."
(Mark 16:20 KJV)

WE MUST BE WILLING
TO STEP OUT IN FAITH

"Now the just shall live by faith: but if any man draw back, my soul shall have no pleasure in him."
(Hebrews 10:38 KJV)

WORSHIP WILL DRAW A CROWD

"And I, if I be lifted up from the earth, will draw all men unto me."
(John 12:32 KJV)

GOD USES ILLUSTRATED SERMONS

"All these things spake Jesus unto the multitude in parables; and without a parable spake he not unto them."
(Matthew 13:34 KJV)

The Word of God tells us, "...he that winneth souls is wise" (Proverbs 11:30 KJV). The Hebrew word for wise is *chakam*, meaning wise, strategic, cunning, crafty, intelligent, skillful, artful, subtle, learned and shrewd.

Choose one or more of these 10 meanings for the word *wise* that you think ties into this testimony.

[ ] wise   [ ] strategic
[ ]cunning   [ ] crafty
[ ] intelligent [ ] skillful
[ ] artful   [ ] subtle
[ ] learned   [ ] shrewd

Validation

Gratefully, my brother Bill led me to the Lord in 1979 and has discipled me on and off throughout the years. It was a blessing to be a part of many episodes concerning evangelism. I am the brother who kept feeding the carni $5 bills at the Lyndsey Fair, where Brother Bill preached his sermon from the top of a car as he beat it with a sledgehammer.

Several years ago, Bill led a revival at our church in Meadville, Pennsylvania. It was great to spend time with him as we reminisced about evangelism episodes we had shared. Brother Bill always left memories with me as we had opportunities to evangelize in different parts of our country—Mardi Gras, New York City, Florida, California to name a few.

Some of these testimonies may seem unbelievable. I have personally witnessed God's power and anointing upon my brother Bill. The experience is always an encouragement to win the lost. Bill has inspired me to lead a street ministry myself—becoming a soul winner on the highways and byways of life.

The stories are true and the names stay the same to uplift the innocent!

Ron Henderson
Bill's brother

CHAPTER 3

Hello, Brazil

In March 1988, I went to Brazil with Arthur Blessitt and a team from the Trinity Broadcasting Network. Our plans were to carry a cross on the beaches of Rio de Janeiro and evangelize a number of places. As we were getting off the airplane, someone handed us a newspaper that read something like this:

> "If you carry the cross on our beach, we will kill you, crucify you, hang you on the cross and sacrifice you to the sea god!"

I remember reading in a magazine on the flight over that a ferryboat cruised up and down the Rio shoreline. I thought to myself, "I didn't come to Brazil to die. All we need to do is get on that ferryboat with some big loud speakers and just like Jesus preached from a boat, we'll preach from a boat too. In a boat we can cover more ground, preach to more people and this will be better."

When we arrived, it was just a few days before the local Brazilians celebrated the Fiesta de Iemanja, the goddess of the sea and mother of the waters. The worshipers of this demon spirit literally remove their watches, rings, wallets and clothing and throw them into the ocean. Then they ask the goddess of the sea to prosper them in the coming year.

We were working with a guy by the name of Jenetto, who was known as one of the greatest evangelists in the country. We ended up doing a meeting in the city of Sao Paolo. While there, we carried the cross. A few days prior to our arrival, in this very neighborhood, a 17-year old had been violently murdered as he handed out gospel tracts. The fact that the main gangster in that area had just gotten saved made our job a lot easier. The result of his conversion was that he ran through the hills ahead of us, commanding the people to come out of their houses and go to hear the gospel through our ministry. In Rio and Sao Paolo, the poor people live in the mountains while the rich people live on the shoreline.

Obey the Lord

Later, in another location, we did a rally on a corner in Sao Paulo where there was a huge Catholic church. We were told that one million people a day crossed that intersection. We set up our stage and speakers and did feats of strength to draw the crowds. While Arthur Blessitt was preaching, he declared to the crowd, "If you are sick, come forward and we will pray for you and our Jesus will heal you right now!" He immediately turned to us and said, "WHAT AM I DOING? WHAT DID I JUST SAY? I'VE NEVER SAID THAT BEFORE! HELP US, JESUS!"

A man on crutches was immediately healed. As soon as Arthur held those crutches in the air, the people swarmed the stage. We prayed for the sick for the next several hours. It was miraculous!

Then one young man walked up to me with his head turned totally sideways. He was tremendously deformed. I didn't know any of the details but as they brought him to the front of the platform, people just pointed to his head.

I looked at him and said, "In the name of Jesus Christ of Nazareth, head be straight!" I pulled his head up straight, then the crowd started jumping, screaming and yelling.

I was wondering what was going on. Then somebody told me, "Did you know he was born like that and his head has never been straight?"

I replied, "Let's give God the glory, people!"

Back in Rio

When we got back to Rio, I found out that our original plan of getting on the boat was not going to work for us. They wouldn't let us on the boat. Our team offered triple the money to get on that boat, but nobody would take it. Remember, they said that they would kill us if we carried the cross on their beach.

So, not being allowed on the boat, we were forced into carrying the cross up and down the shoreline. But the night before we carried the cross, in the face of those overt death threats, we literally laid before God in prayer for a number of hours then took communion. We were preparing to die. We wept, repented, washed each other's feet, and we prayed, "Lord, this is where we get to live out the scripture."

The Bible says, "They overcame him by the blood of the Lamb and the word of their testimony." And that verse ends by saying, "...and they loved not their lives unto the death" (Revelation 12:11-12).

I prayed, "Father, this is where we get to live this. Jesus, I know that we didn't come here to die. I am asking you to deliver us. But, if this is what it takes, we're not gonna tuck tail and run." After prayer, we looked at each other and said, "If we live, we live. But if we die, we die for Jesus."

The next morning we went to the beach with the cross and started to march. Jenetto, a Brazilian evangelist, told us that there were several thousand expected to be on that beach.

Jenetto had advertised the event for a year ahead of time, hoping that all the churches would work together to reach the city with the gospel. He had been encouraging them to march for Jesus and rally around the cross, hoping that people would drop their denominational differences.

The day we marched with the cross on the beach, sure enough, thousands of people turned out. As we marched, we stomped out the voodoo candles that were on the beach. Backslidden Christians were everywhere up and down the beach. Some began to weep from conviction as we were worshipping God. You could hear thousands singing "Jesu," which is "Jesus" in Portuguese.

There were those that came to us saying, "I'm from America and I'm backslidden. I'm out here smoking dope, drinking beer and I feel so horrible."

We would tell them, "Just get in line—man, throw that stuff away and tell the Lord you're sorry." Many repented, jumped in the line and marched with us. Can you imagine? There were thousands and thousands of worshippers for Jesus on the beach that night, singing praises and giving glory to God. Here is an example of God raising up a Radical Remnant!

Boat Mysteriously Capsized

Later on, we found out that the boat we tried to get on had mysteriously capsized. Out of 208 people on board that day, only eight people lived. Tragically, 200 people drowned. Officially, they didn't know why the boat turned over and sank. We believe that the witch doctors and voodoo priests who wrote the "death threat" had something to do with the boat sinking. They must have heard that we were trying to get on the boat. Only eternity will reveal the truth of what happened that day. But go with me now, ten years later, for the rest of the story.

Meet Marcos

In 1998, my wife and I were working with YWAM (Youth With A Mission) and their evangelistic outreach teams in Brazil. This time we were in a city called Forteleza. While we were there ministering for two weeks, Kevin Stark, one of our team leaders, brought a man to me and said, "Bill, meet Marcos." He continued, "He flew here and wants to work with our team." Kevin went on to say, "I'm trying to figure out how to make it work, though. Why don't you talk to him and you make the decision."

I said, "Okay." Turning to Marcos, I said, "What do you do? Do you break bricks? Do you blow up hot water bottles? What do you do?" (These are some of the feats of strength we did to draw a crowd.)

Through our translator, he replied, "No." All of a sudden he removed his glasses, spread his legs, and stood in a karate stance. He began to kick his legs straight up in the air and did circles over my head—missing my face by only inches! Next, he placed a dime on my head and kicked it off without touching my head.

"Wow!" I thought. "This guy is a real live ninja!"

He went on to say the bishop of the church he attended in Sao Paulo told him about us and he wanted to come to Forteleza and meet us and work with us. This bishop was over many churches in Brazil. I noticed as he continued talking to me that he was staring holes through me. Through the translator I said, "Ask him how long he's been doing this form of martial arts."

It turned out he'd been doing Capoeria since he was a child. But as he answered, he continued to stare and never looked away from me even when he began his inquiry of the translator. He asked me, through the translator, if I had been in Sao Paulo ten years ago, doing power feats and preaching.

My reply was, "Yes, I was."

Suddenly tears began to well up in his eyes. He said through the translator that I was the one who led him to the Lord. Since then he had led thousands and thousands to Jesus! He had been praying for ten years to meet me face to face! As he was weeping, he grabbed me, hugged me intensely, and stated, "You are my spiritual father!"

I Came to Kill You

Marcos went on to say, "In the late eighties, you were in Sao Paulo, preaching on a street corner across from a large Catholic church, giving your testimony about how you used to sell drugs and how you were a street fighter. It got my attention and I began to listen. What you don't know, Bill, is that on that day, I came to kill you and those with you."

While we were doing power feats, the townsmen were fast at work making arrangements with the voodoo witch doctors who gave Marcos an assignment. "Go and kill all of those men!" Marcos was accompanied by ten of his martial arts students who were each high degree black belts, but on the way they got into an argument about exactly *how* they were going to kill us. Marcos continued to recount the story. He said, "As I approached the stage that you were on, all of a sudden I felt a hand on my chest that pushed me back down the steps. I started looking around but I could see nothing. But still I could feel a hand on my chest. Then I heard a voice that said, 'Do my servants no harm and listen to them.' I started watching and listening to what was being said as you continued to give your testimony."

After we finished our feats of strength, we then prayed for the sick and God was healing everybody. I can remember that the Holy Spirit's presence was immense and so strong there. Even nonbelievers like Marcos could feel God's presence. Marcos ended up being totally convicted by God. He repented and gave his life to the Lord then and there that very day.

What a powerful testimony! From being an assassin for the devil to a full-blown witness of Jesus. Today Marcos, a master in Capoeria, has led thousands, young and old, to Jesus through his own television program in Brazil called "Capoeria for Jesus." He also has traveled extensively throughout the rest of the world and recently moved to America where he works with YWAM.

Marcos later asked me, "Remember the march you were a part of?"

I replied, "Yeah, how could I forget it?"

Marcos continued, "Never before had we as Christians ever marched with a cross, but from that first Jesus March on the Rio de Janeiro beach in 1988 until now, all the churches come together and march for Jesus every year. Guess how many people march now," Marcos asked.

"How many?" I replied.

He answered with great excitement. "Hundreds of thousands every year!"

So to this very day, they are still marching on that beach after our first march in 1988.

Summary

"Behold, how good and how pleasant it is for brethren to dwell together in unity! It is like the precious ointment upon the head, that ran down upon the beard, even Aaron's beard: that went down to the skirts of his garments; As the dew of Hermon, and as the dew that descended upon the mountains of Zion: for there the Lord commanded the blessing, even life for evermore." (Psalms 133:1-3 KJV)

In the Hebrew, this Psalm means: when many come together all at one time, even though there are differences of opinions and ideas, even if it's negative and stressful. If we simply endure and unite anyway for one purpose, it is there God commands His blessing, His peace, His prosperity, His praise and strength and He causes us to be fresh and revived. It is there God sends His messengers. It is there that He commands and ordains a divine act that sets things in order. This is why the apostolic teamwork is so powerful and prophetic for this end-time harvest.

The Word of God tells us, "...he that winneth souls is wise" (Proverbs 11:30 KJV). The Hebrew word for wise is *chakam*, meaning wise, strategic, cunning, crafty, intelligent, skillful, artful, subtle, learned and shrewd.

Choose one or more of these 10 meanings for the word *wise* that you think ties into this testimony.

[ ] wise   [ ] strategic
[ ] cunning   [ ] crafty
[ ] intelligent   [ ] skillful
[ ] artful   [ ] subtle
[ ] learned   [ ] shrewd

CHAPTER 4

Go to Jamaica and Find God

"But if from thence, thou shalt seek the
Lord thy God, thou shalt find Him, if
thou seek Him with all they heart and
with all thy soul."
(Deuteronomy 4:29 KJV)

One year I was working with a large team in
Jamaica with Pastor Dave Demolia of Faith
Fellowship Church in New Jersey. His inten-
tion was to plant a church solely from the
new converts that gave their lives to Jesus
during our evangelistic efforts. He was holding nightly crusades in Jamaica while we
were teaching street evangelism in the city of
Montego Bay—teaching others how to actually preach on the street.

While we were on the streets, I was intro-
duced to Pastors Jules and Deborah Boquet.
We were teamed to preach together. Pastor
Jules told me that God had called him to be a
street preacher and sent him to Jamaica to
preach on the streets. I asked him where he
was from and he said that he pastored a
church in Houma, Louisiana, called Christian
Community Fellowship, now Harvest Cathedral.

I was a bit apprehensive about him working
with me only because my past experience

with pastors in street evangelism had been difficult. As our days working together went by, Pastor Jules shocked me with his passion and fire to preach to the lost. It was awesome to preach with this radical man from Cajun country.

Later that day while preaching on a flat bed truck, I witnessed the town demoniac getting set free—coming into his right mind and giving his life to Jesus. It was just like reliving the book of Acts.

Rastafarians

The next day we went to a small Rastafarian village. The Rastafarians are religious followers of Haile Selassie, the former emperor and king of Ethiopia. Rastafarians smoke marijuana as a kind of religious sacrament. They call marijuana *ganja*, and as they smoke it, they believe they can contact God.

Pastor Jules, myself and another man who was going to pastor the newly planted church, were in the Rastafarian village made up of huts, houses and little stores where the people made home-crafted items to sell to the tourists. As we went through their shops, we invited them to come down to an open area near the ocean because we had something powerful to tell them.

Pastor Jules began to share the gospel to those who had gathered. He reminded them that just like the Rastafarians were asking us to come through their open doors to shop, God wanted them to come to Him today through His open door. "This open door's name is Jesus," Pastor Jules said and gave an altar call where many came forward.

At that point, I walked up and said to them, "Lo, behold, there is water. What prevents us from being baptized? If you really meant the prayer that you just prayed, to accept Jesus as your Savior, then you will go all the way and take the next step and be water baptized. Even if this brings persecution, God will be with you." Then I said, "Follow me to the water." As I turned my back to them and walked into the water, they began to come one by one. Some, however, were afraid and did not come.

Throughout the day we continued to preach several mini sermons from the water. Also, many guests from the hotel were being drawn to listen to the gospel. Suddenly, a man walked over toward us and asked to be saved and baptized. As he came out of the water, he asked for the bullhorn because he had something to say. Normally, I would never give the microphone to a stranger, but this time I felt compelled to hand it over.

The man began to share that he had come from Tennessee where others had told him that if he would come to Jamaica, he would find God. He had spent all of his money getting to Jamaica and even had to sell his personal belongings to make the trip. He said that there had been some sort of convention in town where he should have been able to find God, but was turned away at the door because he could not afford the twenty-five dollar entry fee.

After being turned away from the convention, in great despair and without any money, he was sleeping on the rocks along the beach. Even the Rastafarians felt sorry for him and gave him table scraps for food. He was in pitiful condition.

Even though he was quite far from where we were baptizing people, he said that he could hear clearly what was being preached. He heard Pastor Jules say, "Many of you came to Jamaica for different reasons, but you really came to Jamaica to find God." This really got his attention.

When he heard those words, he was reminded of what he was told back in Tennessee. "You will find God in Jamaica." Right then he knew that he had to respond to God's voice. Pastor Jules and I led him to Jesus and then baptized him. We were all so moved by his testimony and hunger for God that we took up an offering to help him get back to America. He left that beach a changed man.

The Hills are Ablaze

The following day the street evangelism continued in the hills above the city in a very dangerous area. As Jules and I were preaching with a half-mile hailer, a man approached us and said in his heavy Jamaican accent, "Hey, Mon! Do you see that group of men over there? They do mean you harm." Rather than waiting for them to approach us, we headed for them.

As we witnessed to them about Jesus, God gave us boldness and words of knowledge that disarmed them. No longer did they want to do us harm. In fact, the entire gang, about a dozen men, gave their lives to Jesus in the middle of the street. We were so excited and glad. God had protected us and saved them.

As we looked around, we noticed that Pastor Jules's wife, Deborah, who had been with us, was missing. We began frantically combing the streets and calling out her name. Eventually we located her on the front porch of an old shack made of many different-sized pieces of old boards. We were delighted to find her on the porch leading the lady of that house to the Lord. Written on one of the old boards on this lady's house were these words: "Salvation Come To This Place." Wow! God answered somebody's prayer. How prophetic those words truly were, because salvation *did come* to her house that day.

Summary

THOSE WHO SEEK GOD WILL FIND HIM

"But if from thence thou shalt seek the Lord thy God, thou shalt find Him, if thou seek Him with all thy heart and with all thy soul."
(Deuteronomy 4:29 KJV)

PLACE OF SALVATION

"And the Lord said, Behold, there is a place by me, and thou shalt stand upon a rock." (Exodus 33:21 KJV)

The Word of God tells us, "...he that winneth souls is wise" (Proverbs 11:30 KJV). The Hebrew word for wise is *chakam*, meaning wise, strategic, cunning, crafty, intelligent, skillful, artful, subtle, learned and shrewd.

Choose one or more of these 10 meanings for the word *wise* that you think ties into this testimony.

[ ] wise   [ ] strategic
[ ] cunning   [ ] crafty
[ ] intelligent   [ ] skillful
[ ] artful   [ ] subtle
[ ] learned   [ ] shrewd

CHAPTER 5

Psalm 911

"He that dwelleth in the secret place of the most High shall abide under the shadow of the Almighty."
(Psalm 91:1 KJV)

My wife Mary Ann and I co-pastored for seven months at an Assembly of God church. When the senior pastor resigned, we became the interim pastors overnight. We were really stretched, but it was wonderful. Soon the AG headquarters had found their replacement and we were back on the road of evangelism again.

On our very last day as pastors, we were to preach and then fly out to Phoenix the next day to hold another service. The church gave us a going away party, prayed for us, laid hands on us and sent us back on the road.

My last sermon that day was, "Don't identify with Bill and Mary Ann. Don't identify with any denomination. Instead, identify with Jesus. That alone is what makes you a spiritual, not a carnal person." After the sermon was preached, many of the members in the congregation tried to get us to change our minds and not leave the church. Many were begging us to stay.

Devil's Going to Kill You

One lady approached me and said, "I want to pray for you because the devil's gonna try to kill you." By this time there were only a few people left at our going away reception. We too were just getting ready to go next door and have cake and cookies. My wife Mary Ann was fifty feet from me, talking to some other people and I was all by myself.

I said to the lady with the message, "Please hold that thought. Wait until my wife is standing next to me."

She said, "It's on me so heavy."

I replied, "Please wait until my wife gets here or go get her and bring her over yourself. Then we'll do this."

The lady walked over and tapped Mary Ann on the shoulder. Then she and Mary Ann came back over to me. The woman said, "I had a dream and Satan hates what you do. He's trying to kill you."

I said, "That's nothing new. There've been many attempts on my life. I know the devil wants us. Some threats you hear about and some you don't know about. Some I even find out about years later. However, if there is something special, then we can agree about it in prayer."

Soteria

Then I shared with her about the word salvation. Salvation is actually two Greek words. One word is *sozo* and that's when we come to Jesus. This means we are delivered spiritually, mentally, socially, financially and academically. The other word for salvation is *soteria*. This means that God will protect us by using His angels to save us from all the evil that is in this world.

I said to her, "Let's just claim *soteria*, because we are catching a plane at 6 a.m. tomorrow morning. Maybe Satan wants to try to crash the plane. I don't know."

So we all held hands and prayed, "Lord, I thank you for *soteria*."

Little did I know, not more than forty minutes from that prayer, something would happen. Mary Ann and I left the church in separate cars on the way home.

Mary Ann was sitting in her car a few blocks from our house. I was in my car in back of her, wondering why she was sitting at a green light talking with her mother. I was thinking to myself, "Well, they're just talking." And they were. Actually it was almost like God blinded them to the fact that the light was green. I was about to honk my horn when suddenly a speeding car ran the red light right through that very intersection. Had Mary Ann gone ahead when the light turned green, it would have been horrible. That car was doing every bit of seventy miles per hour. All I could say was, "Whoa, Jesus! Thank you for *soteria*." Later on, Mary Ann told me the Holy Spirit prompted her to wait, even after the light turned green.

It's Party Time

I had no clue that that was only Part A of what was about to happen. We drove a couple of blocks more. Along the way I continued to thank the Lord that he protected my wife and mother-in-law. As we pulled up to our house, there were cars lining the streets. It was nearly 1 a.m. by this time. I was thinking, "Somebody's having a major party." Little did I know it was my Hispanic next-door neighbor who was having the party with his friends.

It seemed that another Latino gang had come to crash the party. When they arrived they were very angry. I never did learn the reason why. A number of teenagers were standing in front of my house and in my driveway and all along my next-door neighbor's driveway too. The entire street was full of cars. Most of the teens were drinking 14 ounce bottles of beer, smoking dope, partying and sniffing glue out of a bag.

As we tried to pull into the drive, we were surrounded by them. At first, I thought that they were going to attack us, but when we pulled into our driveway they just kind of saw that we lived there and ignored us. I pulled in at our duplex at the far end. Mary Ann had pulled into the parking slot closest to where the action was.

We had been having problems with drugs in the area a year before. Because our bedroom faced the street, we had been kept up probably every night for about a year. Our drug-dealing neighbors had visitors coming and going all night. I had once told them, "Hey guys. Do you know it is obvious what you are doing? You need to either give your life to Jesus or change your point of sting operation, because it's getting way too obvious. All the neighbors are talking about it, and they're gonna get together and bust you guys."

But this night, I warned Mary Ann, "Quick! Get in the house now! They are all very high and they mean business." There are a lot of them. When they wear their bandannas half-masking their eyes the way they are, it means "We've come to do war!"

It's Coming Down

Once you see that it's going to happen, someone better quickly call 911. I said, "Mary Ann, get on the phone. Dial 911. Start praying in the Spirit as hard as you can. This is gang violence and it's coming down."

Then I began to hear threatening words like, "Hey, you! Come out of the house man or we're gonna come in and shoot you in the face." Some of them were wagging guns. Some of them had their hands in their coats as if ready to pull guns.

So we started doing some serious praying. I was inside praying furiously in the Spirit as I was looking through the blinds. Meanwhile, as more cars were coming, the crowd outside was getting bigger and more intense. The rival gang members were increasingly yelling obscenities at each other. I was praying intensely, "I rebuke you. You spirit of death. You spirit of violence. I bind you. I cast you out!" I was praying and coming against every demonic force I knew.

All of a sudden, the Lord gave me a vision. In the vision I saw my wife and my mother-in-law on the floor bleeding. Our house had been shot up with bullet holes everywhere. I saw gangs carrying automatic sub-machine guns. I knew then what I had to do. I looked at my wife and I said, "Mary Ann, pray like you never have prayed before. Pray in tongues. I have to do what I have to do."

She questioned, "What do you have to do?"

I replied, "You just pray. I have to obey God." At that point, obeying the Lord's leading was almost like jumping off a diving board. You just jump. You just have to do what He's leading you to do.

I ran out the front door to the corner of the fence and jumped up on top of the fence yelling, "Hey! Hey everybody! I'm right here! Hey! Look at me, look at me!" Some of these gang bangers were looking at me while others tried to ignore me. I said, "You guys are on the wrong side of the fence!"

There was a hush, almost like a Holy Ghost hush, that came on them.

"You guys are on the wrong side of the fence," I repeated. "You need to become...." Right about here, God really took over.

God's Turf

I was kind of talking their slang. "Vatos!" I said. "Look at me. I got tattoos too. I've got tattoos all over my body. I used to do what you guys do. Hey! I used to sell drugs. I used to make drugs. I'll tell you right now, Jesus is the answer you're looking for!" I continued, "A number of years ago, I died of a drug overdose. I cried out and asked Jesus to come in."

I just kept preaching to them. I said, "Now this place is my turf. This is my neighborhood. This place belongs to God. You are not gonna kill nobody. Every spirit of violence, every spirit of interruption that's here, in the name of Jesus, get out of here! Go! And when you go home, think about Jesus. Think about calling on the name of Jesus."

All of a sudden, they started saying, "Okay, okay, okay." They began putting their guns away, got in their cars and drove away. They left like a swarm of ravens.

But it wasn't over yet. They came back a second time. When they returned, it was a repeat, almost like a second performance. When they came back I walked outside and said, "Hey, didn't you hear me the last time? Do you understand? This is my neighborhood. I am a Christian. I love Jesus. This is Jesus' ground."

So I just began to preach to them again. Not yelling. Instead, I used a softer voice. The Lord gave me a word of knowledge about a girl. I looked at this girl and I said, "Young lady, the Lord shows me that your mother is home tonight praying that you'll give your heart to Jesus. He shows me that you are backslidden."

She shouted back at me, "You liar!" She called me a liar to my face, in front of all her friends.

Then all the dudes started swarming around me. I said, "I'm gonna repeat myself.

Your mother loves Jesus and she's praying to Jesus that you would come to Him." God was definitely right there in the midst of this scene.

The girl suddenly dropped her head and said, "He's right."

When everybody heard that, they backed off. When that happened, I was able to talk to them with a whole lot more receptivity. By now, it must have been around two in the morning. Their cars were parked right in front of our house. I poked my head in a car door and was talking to a whole car full of them. A couple of them were standing outside. I said, "Look, guys. Get back in your car and drive down the street. Go home and tell your mothers that somebody who loves Jesus came over to talk to you tonight."

> "He that dwelleth in the secret place of the most High shall abide under the shadow of the Almighty."
> (Psalm 91:1 KJV)

Summary

SPIRITUAL AUTHORITY
> "Behold, I give unto you power to tread on serpents and scorpions, and over all the power of the enemy; and nothing shall by any means hurt you."
> (Luke 10:19 KJV)

WHOM SHALL I FEAR?

"But whoso hearkeneth unto me shall dwell safely, and shall be quiet from fear of evil." (Proverbs 1:33 KJV)

Oftentimes, fear keeps people out of the harvest fields. Let's take a look at some real statistics.

- 60% of fearful things are totally unwarranted and will never happen.

- 20% of our fears comes from what has happened to us in our past. Even though those things are gone and over, they continue to influence the decisions that we make today.

- 10% of our fears are petty and cause us to live in apprehension or are things which cause us to worry about something that will never happen. Even if those fears were to happen, they would not change anything.

- So that leaves us with 10% left to deal with—of which only 4 to 5% has a reality base. The remaining 5 or 6% is really nothing but fearful and vain imaginations.

INTERCESSION

"Likewise the Spirit also helpeth our infirmities; for we know not what we should pray for as we ought; but the Spirit itself maketh intercession for us with groanings which cannot be uttered." (Romans 8:26 KJV)

WORD IS POWERFUL

"For the word of God is quick, and powerful, and sharper than any two-edged sword, piercing even to the dividing asunder of soul and spirit, and of the joints and marrow, and is a discerner of the thoughts and intents of the heart." (Hebrews 4:12 KJV)

The Word of God tells us, "...he that winneth souls is wise" (Proverbs 11:30 KJV). The Hebrew word for wise is *chakam,* meaning wise, strategic, cunning, crafty, intelligent, skillful, artful, subtle, learned and shrewd.

Choose one or more of these 10 meanings for the word *wise* that you think ties into this testimony.

[ ] wise   [ ] strategic
[ ] cunning   [ ] crafty
[ ] intelligent   [ ] skillful
[ ] artful   [ ] subtle
[ ] learned   [ ] shrewd

Validation

My husband, Bill Henderson, is not only passionate in his love for Jesus Christ, but he is compassionate about reaching the lost. Many times I have been convicted in a positive way as I have watched Bill reach out to those who are crying out in their hearts for the reality of God. His faith is so strong that no matter what evil situation may be present, he knows he can overcome it through faith by the word that is written, "greater is He that is in you than he that is in the world." Bill is one of the boldest men I have ever met and yet sensitive to the Holy Spirit. This story and all that are in this book are accounted for and are accurate.

I personally witnessed the 911 incident. These accounts also represent the end results of a true Apostolic Evangelist—winning the lost at any cost.

"The righteous are bold as a lion." (Proverbs 28:1)

That describes Bill Henderson.

Unashamed and bold!

Mary Ann Henderson
Bill's wife

CHAPTER 6

Best Punch at Mardi Gras

"And the Lord said unto the servant,
Go out into the highways and hedges,
and compel them to come in, that my
house may be filled." (Luke 14:23 KJV)

For a number of years now, we've gone to
preach Jesus and win souls during the
weeklong Mardi Gras celebration in New
Orleans. Once we were in the French Quarter
and my dad, who had recently been saved,
was with me. Having heard so much about
my lifestyle of evangelism, my dad was excited to go out with me and be a part of the
great things that Jesus was doing.

I said, "Okay now Dad, if you're gonna do
this, then you gotta do this right. I have been
teaching on evangelism for years. Here is
something that you can do today to help me
win souls, and learn at the same time. This is
one of many ways that we reach people when
there are large noisy crowds. Take this big
speaker—we call it a half-mile hailer—and
put it on top of your head."

Dad said in a Cajun accent, "Yeah, that's
all I've got to do is just put that on my head."

I said, "That's right, Dad. Just hold it on
your head. Oh, and just one more thing. As
we walk down through the crowd, I want you

to pan left, slowly turn the bullhorn's speaker for thirty seconds to the left, and then pan right for thirty seconds. Can you remember to do that?"

"Can I remember to do that?" he replied. "Sure! An idiot can do that! Pan left and right every thirty seconds. Sure enough, yeah, I can do that!"

I said, "Oh Dad, one final thing. This bullhorn costs several hundred dollars. So I want you to hang onto this thing like you're laying block! Don't drop it. Pretend like you're laying blocks and there's a little old lady walking below you and if you drop it you will kill her. Don't drop the bullhorn whatever you do. Okay, Dad? Squeeze it and don't let go of it. Don't let anybody steal it. Don't drop it. Got it?"

Again Dad responded in his Cajun Louisiana accent, "Yeah, yeah, I got it son. You know, it's a piece of cake. Y'know I'll hang onto that thing like I was part of it, like it was my head or something!"

Devil's Best Shot

We walked for 15 minutes down the packed street. I've got this extra long extension cord so Dad was about 20 feet in front of me. I was watching him panning left and panning right, panning left and panning right. All of a sudden I heard somebody shout, "You no good blankety-blank." Then I saw a guy running wildly out of a bar. I mean he was running full bore, like a wild animal charging its prey.

I was maybe 20 to 25 feet behind Dad and I shouted, "Dad! Look out! Look to your right!" My dad was holding the half-mile hailer on his head. I was preaching and this running man was screaming obscenities and heading straight at my dad. Then, suddenly, he punched my dad right in the face, SMACK!

My dad began to stagger, bob and weave like a hula-hoop girl in the back window of a 1950 Chevy. It was a TKO but Dad was still on his feet. Because of the pep talk I had given him, somehow, unbelievably, he did not let go of that loud speaker! I remember saying, "Help him, Jesus!" as I ran over to him and grabbed him.

Dad looked like a frog in a rainstorm. He was batting his eyes, saying, "What WAS that? What happened son?"

I said, "Dad, a guy just smacked you in the jaw with everything he had. Awesome, Dad! I am proud of you. I can't believe you didn't drop the speaker!"

Ready to Rumble

Dad shouted, "What did he do that for? All you were saying was that God loved them and that Jesus died for them." Then, as Dad began to feel the pain, he said, "Here, hold this speaker. Hold this thing! Which way did he go?" He was fighting mad and ready to rumble.

I said, "Dad, listen to me. Jesus is watching. If you will forgive that man right now, I promise you that you're gonna get a star in your crown in heaven for taking that punch." I couldn't think of any other words to say to him because I was trying to put it in his language.

Then, all of a sudden, Dad said, "Oh, yeah! A star huh?"

I could see Dad opening and closing his jaw to make sure that it wasn't broken. Then Dad said, "Son, I'll tell you what. I mean this from the bottom of my heart. I don't think I could handle too many stars in one day."

Amidst my laughter, I said, "Dad, you're really gonna get that star!"

Later my dad told me that he had a great respect for me and anyone who would take the gospel to events such as Mardi Gras. That day my dad learned about the power of forgiveness. I was reminded that in the ministry of reconciliation, there is always *opposition with intensity.*

> "And all things are of God, who hath reconciled us to himself by Jesus

Christ, and hath given to us the ministry of reconciliation."
(II Corinthians 5:18 KJV)

Summary

COMPEL THEM TO COME IN

"And the Lord said unto the servant,
Go out into the highways and hedges,
and compel them to come in, that my
house may be filled." (Luke 14:23 KJV)

The Greek word for compel is *anagkazo*
meaning to agitate, drive to and constrain by
force or other means.

WE WRESTLE NOT AGAINST
FLESH AND BLOOD

"For we wrestle not against flesh and
blood, but against principalities,
against powers, against the rulers of
the darkness of this world, against
spiritual wickedness in high places."
(Ephesians 6:12 KJV)

BLESS THOSE THAT CURSE YOU

"But I say unto you, Love your en-
emies, bless them that curse you, do
good to them that hate you, and pray
for them which despitefully use you,
and persecute you."
(Matthew 5:44 KJV)

TURN THE OTHER CHEEK

"But I say unto you, That ye resist not evil; but whosoever shall smite thee on thy right cheek, turn to him the other also." (Matthew 5:39 KJV)

FORGIVENESS

"And when ye stand praying, forgive, if ye have ought against any; that your Father also which is in heaven may forgive you your trespasses."
(Mark 11:25 KJV)

The Word of God tells us, "...he that winneth souls is wise" (Proverbs 11:30 KJV). The Hebrew word for wise is *chakam*, meaning wise, strategic, cunning, crafty, intelligent, skillful, artful, subtle, learned and shrewd.

Choose one or more of these 10 meanings for the word *wise* that you think ties into this testimony.

[ ] wise	[ ] strategic
[ ] cunning	[ ] crafty
[ ] intelligent	[ ] skillful
[ ] artful	[ ] subtle
[ ] learned	[ ] shrewd

CHAPTER 7

The Chase

"So shall my word be that goeth forth
out of my mouth: it shall not return
unto me void, but it shall accomplish
that which I please, and it shall prosper *in the thing* whereto I sent it."
(Isaiah 55:11 KJV)

One afternoon I was driving my van down a
long mountain road in East Highlands, California. It was on the very same road that I
learned how to drive. My mom used to take
me up there when I was thirteen, fourteen
and fifteen—down this long, extremely de-
serted two-lane road. It had one lane that
went one way, and one lane that went the
other. It was a winding road with dips, hills
and very narrow bridges. The road was often
traveled by drug dealers and those who like
to party.

So one day while I was driving, I looked in
my rear view mirror only to see this car getting ready to pass me. It looked like it could
be doing maybe 100 miles an hour. I was
driving 50 to 60 miles an hour because I
knew the road really well. I saw a bit of a
curve up ahead and another car coming our
way. I calculated very quickly that if I just
stayed put, by the time the driver passed me,
he would hit this other car head on. So I
quickly pulled off the road and let him go by.

It was difficult because there was really no-where to pull off the road, so my van shud-dered as I pulled off onto the very rough semi-shoulder.

The guy flew on by me and I realized that I had saved that guy's life. I got back on the road and started driving along when I saw the car that had just passed me pulled over on the shoulder. There was a bunch of people inside, maybe five or six. I could see that they were drinking and using the side of the road as their restroom.

I passed them and I almost stopped to witness to them, but instead I just prayed for them. "Lord, send the laborers of the harvest into their lives." After all, I had an appoint-ment that I was going to. I was on my way to see my pastor. About 10 minutes down the road, I saw in the rear view mirror the same car coming up fast behind me again. Same thing, he was doing about 100 miles an hour and driving crazy. I had a repeat of the same scenario—if I didn't move over, he was going to hit somebody head on.

So off the shoulder of the road I went again. Vrrooom!!! He passed me by but this time I prayed, "Lord, somebody has to reach this guy."

The Lord responded and said to me, "You're that somebody."

I put the gas pedal to the floor. My van had a big 360 motor and though my van was big and heavy, it was quick. So as I speeded up, I prayed, "Lord, help me catch this guy."

For the next few minutes I was on this guy's tail. He'd pass a car and I'd pass a car. He'd pass two cars and I'd pass two right behind him. The chase was on. Everything he did, I did. It was INTENSE! I hate to admit this, but we were both really exceeding the speed limit.

I was thinking, "I'm not letting you get away! I don't care what it takes. I'm gonna catch you in Jesus' name!" Then I began praying, "Lord, help me catch him. This guy is just like the old Bill Henderson. He is exactly how I used to be because I too would run people off the road and didn't even care. God, please help me catch this guy. Please don't let us crash." I was praying the whole time I was chasing this guy. I prayed, "Lord, keep your hand on us both."

Now we were approaching a hairpin turn. It was an incredibly hard right. To make it safely, we would have to slow down to maybe 25 miles an hour max, or risk flipping over. As I began to slow down, he didn't. I was thinking, "Oh my God, he's not going to make it. Lord, there's no way he can make that turn. He's going too fast."

As he began to pull away from me, I was ready to watch him roll over and crash. To my surprise, instead of trying to make the turn, he just went straight ahead off the main road and onto a dirt road. I didn't make the turn in the road either. I followed him along the dirt road. I punched the gas and kicked it into all four barrels. The chase was still on.

So I was chasing him on a dirt road for the next 7 or 8 minutes. Dust, rocks and dirt were flying everywhere. The rocks were hitting my window. I could hardly see the car in front of me because there was so much dust. But I was still right on his tail.

Because I knew the road so well, I was thinking, "This road dead ends at a mountain in just a minute. He's got to stop then." I prayed, "Lord, don't let him get out and run away. Make him stay in the car." Sure enough, you could hear a *whoosh* as the driver jammed on his brakes and skidded sideways to a complete stop.

Life and Death, You Choose

Because I was going so fast, I hit my brakes in an attempt to avoid crashing into him. Thank God, my van stopped just a few feet from him. When all the dust and smoke settled, I could see him from my van. I was just sitting there looking at him and his carload of people. I was praying in the Spirit and asking the Lord what I should do next.

I reached down inside my van where I kept my Bible. I put my Bible behind my back, opened up my van door, and started to walk toward his car. The driver could not see what was behind my back. I walked over to him in a crouched and sideways position. I had a stern look on my face. I pointed at him with my finger and as I got closer and closer with one hand still behind my back, I was praying, "Lord, give me the right words to say."

As I drew closer to him, I could tell that there was a whole carload of teenagers with him. They were frozen like mannequins, staring at me and wondering what I was going to do next. I looked at him and said, "You ran me off the road twice! Behind my back is life and death, blessing and cursing." In a loud voice, I said, "Young man, you choose!" Then, for just a moment, there was dead silence as he stared at me in horror. Then he said slowly with fear and trembling in his voice, "I choose life."

All those in the car were saying, "Life, sir. We want life!"

Then I pulled out my Bible from behind my back and said, "Good! Because Jesus said I am the way, the truth, and the life. He also said whosoever shall call on the name of the Lord shall be saved."

I looked at the driver and said, "Young man, you need to call on Jesus." Then the girl sitting next to him took her elbow and began to continually hit him. Wham! Wham! I asked the girl, "Why are you doing that?" The driver just stared straight ahead.

She said, "I am his sister and you sound just like our mother. Our mother said that someday somebody just as crazy as my brother was gonna come into his life and tell him that he needs Jesus. And today I just saw the answer to her prayers."

One of the young people in the back seat thought I was going to kill them all and was very happy when the driver chose life. At that point, I led all of them in a prayer calling on Jesus.

I learned a powerful lesson that day. God answered that mother's prayer. God always sends somebody, and that day I was that somebody.

Summary

PRAYERS ARE RELEASED
INTO OUR FUTURES

> "So shall my word be that goeth forth out of my mouth: it shall not return unto me void, but it shall accomplish that which I please, and it shall prosper in the thing whereto I sent it."
> (Isaiah 55:11 KJV)

ENVANGELISM IS NEVER CONVENIENT

"Preach the word; be instant in season, out of season; reprove, rebuke, exhort with all longsuffering and doctrine." (II Timothy 4:2 KJV)

In season and out of season means to preach in favorable or unfavorable conditions.

NEVER GIVE UP ON YOUR LOVED ONES

"And they said, Believe on the Lord Jesus Christ, and thou shalt be saved, and thy house." (Acts 16:31 KJV)

The Word of God tells us, "...he that winneth souls is wise" (Proverbs 11:30 KJV). The Hebrew word for wise is *chakam*, meaning wise, strategic, cunning, crafty, intelligent, skillful, artful, subtle, learned and shrewd.

Choose one or more of these 10 meanings for the word *wise* that you think ties into this testimony.

[ ] wise   [ ] strategic
[ ] cunning   [ ] crafty
[ ] intelligent [ ] skillful
[ ] artful   [ ] subtle
[ ] learned   [ ] shrewd

CHAPTER 8

Bus Station Angels

"Be not forgetful to entertain strangers: for thereby some have entertained angels unawares." (Hebrews 13:2 KJV)

I was traveling across the country with my friend and disciple Tim Vandervere. After reaching Colorado Springs, where I stopped off to see my younger brother Tim, I continued traveling to Deming, New Mexico. After spending some time with my brother, I led him to Jesus. A few days later I got back on the bus to catch up with my traveling companion.

The trip to Deming, New Mexico, took hours and hours. The bathroom on the bus was out of order and I had a desperate need to use the bathroom. To help pass the time, I had been reading through Dr. Billy Graham's book called *Angels, Angels, Angels.* I was fascinated with this unseen army of angels that he wrote about. Especially the scripture in II Kings: 6:16 where Elisha prayed, "Lord open Gehazi's eyes." Gehazi was Elisha's servant and God did open his eyes to see that "those that are with us are more than those that are with them." Gehazi saw the mountainside filled with flaming chariots of angels of the Most High God.

A Thousand Angels

At last the bus stopped at Albuquerque. As everyone was getting off the bus, I was thinking I knew where they were all going. Because of the crowd, I thought, "Well, I've waited this long. I can wait a little longer." As I sat back down on the bus and waited, I read a little more about the angels in the book. I had all these thoughts about angels going through my mind. I remember praying, "Father, in the name of Jesus, I ask for a thousand angels to go into this bus station with me. Let's promote the Kingdom of God!" Heading for the bathroom, I thought, "Wow, I wonder what's gonna happen now!"

In those days I looked pretty wild. I was newly saved and had really long hair and a beard. My teeth needed extensive dental work and I was wearing a Levi leather motorcycle jacket with the sleeves cut off and the backside lined with silver rivets. Even though the coat was tattered and frayed on the sleeves, it was my favorite jacket. To look at me, you might never have known that I was saved.

Give Me the Coat, Man

So I hurried into the bathroom looking like a biker. As I stood there using the facilities, I felt a tap on my shoulder. As I turned and looked, all I could see was a straight razor going bang, bang, bang on my right shoulder. Then I heard this guy say, "Hey, dude." His face came along side of mine. He looked to me like he was high on LSD. He had that classic demon-possessed biker look in his eyes. He had a wild grin and a sadistic kind of laugh.

He said to me, "I like your coat man and I want it!"

I said, "That's nice, but it's my favorite coat. I've had it a lot of years and I don't intend on giving it to anybody."

Then he opened his straight razor so I could see the blade showing. He tapped me again with the knife and said, "Hey dude, I want your coat NOW," as he continued to tap me on my neck and shoulder. Ask yourself what you would be doing or thinking in a situation like this.

At that split second I thought to myself, "Do I punch him or do I pray?" I must admit that I really wanted to handle it the way the old Bill Henderson would handle it. All kinds of thoughts were racing through my mind. I thought, "First I'll hit him with a back fist and while he's stunned, I'll get myself together and side kick him." Then I recalled a scripture that I had recently learned, "And him that taketh away thy cloak, forbid not to take thy coat also. Give to every man that asketh of thee; and of him that taketh away thy goods ask them not again" (Luke 6:29-30).

As I quickly finished nature's call, I turned and took off my coat and threw it at him.

Now it was just he and I in the bathroom. As I continued to speak to him, I noticed that he was looking behind me and all around me with a look of fear on his face. I said, "Listen, dude, you don't intimidate me. As a matter of fact, I used to fight ten guys like you at a time. So I'm not afraid of you at all. If this would have happened just a few months ago, you and I would be outside and I'd be mopping up the parking lot with your face!" I continued, "But I want you to know that I have accepted Jesus Christ as my Savior and I am now a born-again Christian."

As I walked toward him, he backed up. He stopped looking at me and continued to back up and look all around the bathroom with a look of terror and panic on his face. I thought to myself as I watched him back up, "He is really hallucinating. He must be just plain stoned out of his mind on acid (LSD). There is no telling what he is looking at." So I just kept on preaching Jesus Christ to him and telling my testimony. Then he suddenly ran out of the bathroom with my jacket in hand.

I was praying, "Man! Lord, I asked for a thousand angels and I got a devil's angel instead." I was so thankful that I didn't get hurt that I literally got on my knees by myself in that bathroom and prayed, "Jesus, I'm asking you to help me reach this man. I'm gonna try to go find him. I claim his soul for your kingdom. In Jesus' name, the devil can't have him. Amen."

Eyes of Fire

I also prayed for someone to be sent to help. I prayed, "I'm gonna try to go and find the guy. Lord, I need another believer, somebody to agree with me." I stood up and walked out of the bathroom and as God is my witness, about 75 feet away I made eye contact with an elderly man. The man's eyes were captivating. I was wondering why I was looking at him so intently. It seemed as if I could not take my eyes off of him. At first I thought that he was trying to hypnotize me. As I continued to look at him, he continued to look at me. I tried to look in another direction, but I couldn't. It was really a strange thing.

The man was dressed in all black. His clothes looked like the kind of outfit that the Amish people wear. He had a big beard that grew upwards and had soul-piercing blue eyes. I had never seen such on-fire blue eyes in my entire life. They were literally eyes of fire!

The strange man grinned and nodded at me. I smiled back at him. As he looked down I followed his glance and noticed that he had a big family Bible on his lap. It was the kind that you would see on your grandmother's coffee table.

I prayed, "Thank you, Jesus! I have some-body to agree in prayer with me." Jesus promised us that, "if two of you shall agree on earth as touching any thing that they shall ask, it shall be done for them of my Father which is in heaven." (Matthew 18:19 KJV) This scripture brought me hope.

I then made a beeline over to the man and said, "Excuse me. You're a believer aren't you?" He smiled real big but never said a word. He just nodded his head and grinned. I said, "If you don't mind my interrupting you, I just had an encounter with a guy that pulled a knife on me in the bathroom and he took my coat. I would really like you to agree with me in prayer because I am gonna try to find this guy so I can reach him. Will you pray and agree with me?" He nodded his head yes.

So I reached over and grabbed the man's hand and prayed, "Father, in the Name of Jesus, I ask you to help me find this guy." While I was praying, I recognized a familiar tap on my shoulder. As I turned around, I was surprised to see that it was the same guy who took my jacket.

But something was different about him. Miraculously he looked like he was in his right mind. He was wearing my coat and it looked like he had even combed his hair. He was definitely in his right mind.

The Biker's Creed

He said to me, "You gave me your coat, now take this in return." He then handed me his razor knife. It was a gold plated antique straight razor—the same kind that people shave with.

Again he said, "Take this."

I remembered the biker's creed. In the biker culture, if somebody wants something from someone, then they must also give that person something in return. They usually will swap their women, guns, or drugs, but the code is that you never take something for nothing. So I was thinking, "He's a biker and because I gave him my coat, he thinks that he has to give me something too." So I told him, "Look, I gave you my coat because I love Jesus. You don't have to give me anything back."

He said forcefully, "I want you to have this!"

So I said, "Okay, I'll take it under one condition. I want to talk to you for a couple of minutes."

He said, "Go ahead."

I looked over at the Amish man who was sitting there with his big forty-pound Bible in his lap. His eyes were saying, "Go for it!"

So there we were, all three of us sitting together. I began to tell the biker that Jesus died on the cross, shed his lifeblood for me and for him. I was reading out of a little tract called *The Four Spiritual Laws* when suddenly the biker said, "Stop!" He then reached into his back pocket and pulled out a Gideon Bible that was shaped like a wallet. He obviously had had it in his back pocket a long time. It was one of those little Bibles, green in color and really tattered. It even had a marker in it. As he handed it to me, he said, "Open it to the marker."

I was thinking, "Okay."

Angels Unaware

I thought I would just play along so I opened up his Gideon New Testament. He said, "Read me what is underlined."

As I turned to the part that was bookmarked, I read, "Do not forget to entertain strangers, for by so doing some have unwittingly entertained angels." (Hebrews 13:2 NKJV) I added, "That's nice. That's pretty good. Is this your favorite scripture?"

Then he pulled up his sleeve and showed me a tattoo on his arm. The tattoo was of a skull and crossbones that read, "Hell's Angels, Albuquerque, New Mexico." Then I thought, "Boy is he confused. This man

thinks that he is some kind of an angel."
Then I said, "Nice tattoo. Nice scripture. Can I
finish now?"

Then he took his little Bible from me and
put it back into his pocket and he said, "Go
ahead and finish your sermon."

I was thinking, "What a distraction," as I
continued preaching to him out of my tract.
At the end of the tract, I was ready to lead
him to Jesus, but he stopped me again and
said, "Can I pray now?"

I replied, "Are you sincere?"

He said, "Yes, I'm sincere. My mother has
been talking to me about Jesus for a long
time."

I said, "Okay."

So I handed him the tract and then he
prayed this prayer out loud all by himself.
"Lord Jesus, I need you. Thank you for dying
on the cross for my sins."

While he was praying, I looked over to see if
the Amish man was looking on. I was thinking, "Can you believe this?" when I noticed
that he was gone. The Amish man with all his
luggage and guitar case had just disap-
peared! The biker continued praying the
sinner's prayer and as he prayed, I stood up

and looked around the bus terminal for the Amish man, but he was nowhere in sight. He had simply vanished.

I was wondering, "Where did that man go?" I sat back down as the biker was still praying. When he finished, he started to weep and cry. I put my arm around him and asked, "Did you really mean that prayer?"

He replied, "Yes, I did."

Last Call for Deming

As we were talking I heard the announcement for the last call to Deming, New Mexico, over the speaker. But because the biker was so touched by the Lord and was in tears, I decided to miss my bus, stay with him and talk some more about Jesus. I asked him if he wanted to grab a bite to eat. He said, "I would love to do that."

Over dinner, I asked him to tell me more of his story. He told me that when he was a kid, he went to church but got in with the wrong crowd and ended up joining the Hell's Angels. He had been running from God for a long time, but something powerful happened to him that day.

He said, "When I put your coat on, something strange happened to me. I just had to come back and talk to you."

"Well," I told him, "that coat is yours, man, from now on and so is Jesus. Wear it with a smile. I commission you to go tell people about Jesus." I gave him a whole stack of the *Four Spiritual Laws* tracts and he took them with a smile.

We were just about done with dinner and my next bus was ready to board. I had been with the biker for about five hours. We had talked about everything. The biker told me that he was going to go and see his mom because he wanted to tell her that he had finally given his life to Jesus. I told him that he needed to get himself into a good church too.

As I started to leave to board my bus, he turned around and asked, "By the way, where are all of your big buddies?"

I said, "What big buddies?"

He said, "You know. Those big buffed guys that were with you."

I repeated, "What big buffed buys? What are you talking about?"

"Don't give me that, man," he demanded. " All your friends in the bathroom. All the big buffed guys. Where did they go?"

I replied, "There wasn't anybody in the bathroom except you and me."

"Hey don't kid me, those guys had huge muscles and were bigger than you." He continued, "They were huge, man. There was a whole bathroom full of them with you."

I thought maybe he had been hallucinating or something so I said, "If I told you who they were, you wouldn't believe me."

So as I boarded my bus to catch up with my friend in Deming, I said one last good bye to the biker.

Months later as I was telling this story, the Spirit of God spoke to me and brought to my mind the scripture in Hebrews 13. "Be careful to entertain strangers because some have entertained angels unawares."

I had forgotten that I had been reading the book about angels by Dr. Billy Graham and had asked for their presence on my way into the bus station that day. It dawned on me what really had happened in the bathroom that day with the biker. The Lord opened my eyes. The biker saw the angels that God had sent to be with me. He described them as the big buffed guys. Looking back now, I think that the Amish man himself must have been an angel too. What do you think?

Summary

THE LORD PROVIDES
ANGELIC ASSISTANCE

"Are they not all ministering spirits,
sent forth to minister for them who
shall be heirs of salvation?"
(Hebrews 1:14 KJV)

ANGELS HAVE CHARGE OVER YOU

"For he shall give his angels charge
over thee, to keep thee in all thy ways."
(Psalms 91:11 KJV)

ANGELS LISTEN
AND RESPOND TO THE WORD

"Bless the LORD, ye his angels, that
excel in strength, that do his com-
mandments, hearkening unto the voice
of his word." (Psalms 103:20 KJV)

The Word of God tells us, "...he that
winneth souls is wise" (Proverbs 11:30 KJV).
The Hebrew word for wise is *chakam*, meaning wise, strategic, cunning, crafty, intelligent, skillful, artful, subtle, learned and
shrewd.

Choose one or more of these 10 meanings for the word *wise* that you think ties into this testimony.

[ ] wise   [ ] strategic
[ ] cunning   [ ] crafty
[ ] intelligent   [ ] skillful
[ ] artful   [ ] subtle
[ ] learned   [ ] shrewd

CHAPTER 9

Chimney Sweep Bob

"The fool hath said in his heart, There is no God." (Psalms 14:1 KJV)

I went to Big Bear Lake in California to witness to a guy named Bob who was a chimney sweep. He was an out-and-out atheist. After three hours of telling him about my conversion, Bob said, "Bill, you know you're an exciting guy and your stories are great, but I'm an atheist and you will never convert me."

I said to Bob, "I am gonna tell you a couple of things before I walk out the door. Number one, the Bible says that the fool says in his heart there is no God. (Psalms 14:1) Then I showed him a tattoo of Jesus' face on my hand with three words that were written over Jesus' head. What does it say Bob?" I asked him to read it out loud.

Bob read, "Jesus is Lord."

I said, "My prayer, Bob, is that this tattoo follows you until you give your life to Jesus." Bob didn't say one word. He just stared at me and then I left.

Five years later, I came back up to Big Bear Lake to attend the God Bless America Festival. I had just finished carrying my cross in the parade and was walking across the park, when a man came running toward me at full speed. The man had a look on his face like either he knew me or had something up his sleeve. He had a great big smile. As he got closer, he jumped in the air, leaping into my arms. I had to catch him. He wrapped his arms around me and kissed me on the cheek. He said, "Bill, I have been praying that I would see you again."

I replied, "Do I know you?"

He said, "It's me, Bob, Bob!"

"Bob? Bob who?" I asked. "Bob the chimney sweep? Bob the bar fighter? Bob the atheist?"

He said, "No! Bob the born-again, spirit-filled, devil-casting-out, bar-witnessing, radical believer! Billy, I'm washed in the blood! I'm saved! I'm sanctified, man!" He began to tell me his story.

He went on to tell me that after I had last seen him, everywhere he went he would see an image of that little Jesus tattoo on my hand—even in his dreams. Even when taking a shower, he would see the tattoo as he would reach for a bar of soap. Somehow he would see a huge Jesus' face in the shower with him, just like the image of the tattoo. He told me that even as he was driving down the mountain, he would either hear "Jesus is

Lord" or he would see the image of that Jesus tattoo. He told me that for five years, the image of Jesus' face on that tattoo followed him. It was in his dreams. It was everywhere.

He told me he had gone to a horror movie like *The Exorcist.* After he left the movie, he got in his truck to drive home on the I-10 freeway near Redlands, California. Suddenly, that same Jesus face tattoo appeared again in the truck. Bob heard a voice too that said, "Bob, if there's something so extremely wicked as what you just saw at the show, don't you think there's something that is the exact opposite?"

Leave Me the Hell Alone

These were Bob's exact words to me. He said that he screamed at the top of his lungs, "Okay, God. Okay, Jesus. If you are real, either come into my heart right now and save me or leave me the hell alone!" During the next few seconds as he was driving, he said that the presence of God filled his automobile. He felt hope and unconditional love surround him. He said that both his hands were shaking so badly that he couldn't even drive. He barely got his vehicle off to the side of the freeway where he began to weep and cry. The next thing he knew, he was praying, "Thank you, Jesus! You are real. You are in my heart. You saved me. I can't believe it. You are real! I'm saved, Jesus! Thank you. Thank you, God!"

Bob told me that he was weeping and crying so much that he could barely see. As he was experiencing the presence of the Holy Spirit and crying, a motorcycle cop pulled up to the truck and motioned for him to roll down the window. As Bob rolled down the window, the cop asked, "Sir, are you okay?"

Bob responded, "Yes, officer, I'm okay. I just accepted Jesus as my personal Lord and Savior and I'm very happy."

The cop said, "Oh, okay," and drove off on his motorcycle. Bob continued crying and praising the Lord for saving his life. Bob said that he sat on the shoulder of the freeway for about an hour while composing himself before he drove home. On his way home, he prayed, "God, please send Bill back into my life." Bob told me that he never was followed by that Jesus tattoo ever again.

Later I had the privilege of performing my first wedding for Bob and his new bride. Of course Bob had a lot of his old bar buddies present and at the end of the service I led many in a prayer to receive the same Jesus that had changed Brother Bob so much. Amen!

Summary

"Where there is no vision, the people perish: but he that keepeth the law, happy is he." (Proverbs 29:18 KJV)

The word vision is the Greek word *chazown* meaning a prophetic word, dream, open-eyed vision, or the reading or understanding of scripture. Even though Bob said that he was an atheist, the Holy Spirit used the image of the Jesus tattoo to continually bring conviction into Bob's life. God truly uses the foolish things to confound the wise. (I Corinthians 1:27)

The Word of God tells us, "...he that winneth souls is wise" (Proverbs 11:30 KJV). The Hebrew word for wise is *chakam*, meaning wise, strategic, cunning, crafty, intelligent, skillful, artful, subtle, learned and shrewd.

Choose one or more of these 10 meanings for the word *wise* that you think ties into this testimony.

[ ] wise   [ ] strategic
[ ] cunning   [ ] crafty
[ ] intelligent   [ ] skillful
[ ] artful   [ ] subtle
[ ] learned   [ ] shrewd

CHAPTER 10

PA Convictions

"And they overcame him by the blood of
the Lamb, and by the word of their
testimony; and they loved not their
lives unto the death."
(Revelations 12:11 KJV)

Take Him to the Streets

Take Him to the Streets, by Jonathan
Gainsbrugh, was a book that I read in my
early Christian walk. I applied what I read
and soon God gave me more. One of the
things that the book taught was to put a PA
system in your vehicle. I installed one under
the hood of my pickup truck and one on my
motorcycle. I would use the PA system in my
truck mainly at stoplights.

One day while sitting in my truck at a
stoplight, I saw a man on the side of the road
working on his truck. I could see him standing on the front bumper of the truck with the
hood up and reaching way under the hood. I
picked up the microphone of the PA system
and said, "God loves you and has a plan for
your life." It so startled him that he raised up
his head and cracked it against the hood.
Coming out from under the hood, jumping
down from the bumper and standing on his
feet, he rubbed his head in pain. Because of

my PA system, he could not tell where the sound was coming from, but he was looking all around and even up to the sky.

I said, "Sir, do you know that if you ask Jesus to come into your heart, he will?" The guy literally held open wide both hands as I saw him begin to pray. I just couldn't stand it any longer. I had to get out of my truck and meet this man. I told him, "It looked like you were praying." He replied that God had just spoken to him from heaven and that he was praying. He went on to tell me that he was destitute and that he had just spent his last change calling churches looking for help. His wife and kids and everything that they owned were in that truck.

I really believed that day was a divine appointment for this man whose name was Archie. I took Archie and his family to my church where God performed a miracle. The church received an offering for him and his family. Enough money came in to purchase another vehicle, put them in an apartment, and still there was money left over. I am happy to say that they became soul-winning members of the church.

There are many stories that I could tell of the effectiveness of winning members for the church. There are many stories I could tell of the effectiveness of using a PA system to preach the gospel on the streets. Here is a story of using the PA on my motorcycle.

The Big Flush

I was trying to win Larry's soul for the Lord. Early one evening, my son and I pulled up in front of his apartment house which positioned my bike so my high beams were shining right into his windows. Leaving my bike running and in an authoritarian voice, I said on my PA, "The house is surrounded! Come out of the house with your hands up! Come out of the house! Walk backwards with your hands over your heads now. You have 60 seconds."

My son whispered in my ear, "Gee, Dad, I hope they don't have guns in there!"

I said to him, "I know they probably have drugs in there but I'm trying to bring them hope to replace their dope." Then I said over the PA with even more force in my voice, "You have 30 seconds to come out of the house!"

Even though my motorcycle was idling, you could hear all the toilets flushing. Then the front door swung open and six men backed out with their hands on top of their heads. I said, "Keep your hands high in the air! Raise your hands higher! And begin to praise the Lord!"

Their response was, "What the XXXX is going on?" as they lowered their hands. They were so angry with me that it could have been my last sermon using a PA system if my son had not been with me.

I got off my bike and went inside with them and said, "I know that you have been doing dope, but I am bringing you hope." I handed all of them gospel tracts and shared personal testimony of my past lifestyle that was similar to their present one. Shortly afterwards and somewhat puzzled, they all left except Larry, the apartment owner.

My friend Larry said to me, "You are crazy, man! You are really crazy! Those guys that just left would cut your throat for thirty-five cents! I don't believe that you are still alive."

At that moment, my son asked, "Dad, can we please go home now?"

I don't know what happened to those guys, but afterwards, Larry told me that God showed him that His kingdom was real through my boldness and my changed life. Just a few days later I led Larry to Jesus. He proceeded to become a great soul-winner.

The Word says, "And they overcame him by the blood of the Lamb, and by the word of their testimony..." (Revelation 12:11 KJV). To overcome means to subdue, conquer, prevail, overwhelm and get the victory. Truly there is power to overcome with our personal testimony. You might feel that this is radical evangelism, but really it is simply normal Christian living. The remainder of this verse says, "and they loved not their lives unto the death."

Summary

POWER TO WITNESS

"But ye shall receive power, after that the Holy Ghost is come upon you: and ye shall be witnesses unto me both in Jerusalem, and in all Judaea, and in Samaria, and unto the uttermost part of the earth." (Acts 1:8 KJV)

The Greek word for witness is *martus*. From that word we get the English word martyr, meaning a passion that is willing to even die for the advancement of the gospel.

HAPPY ENDING FOR ARCHIE AND FAMILY

"For I know the thoughts that I think toward you, saith the Lord, thoughts of peace, and not of evil, to give you an expected end. Then shall ye call upon me, and ye shall go and pray unto me, and I will hearken unto you. And ye shall seek me, and find me, when ye shall search for me with all your heart." (Jeremiah 29:11-13 KJV)

The Word of God tells us, "...he that winneth souls is wise" (Proverbs 11:30 KJV). The Hebrew word for wise is *chakam*, meaning wise, strategic, cunning, crafty, intelligent, skillful, artful, subtle, learned and shrewd.

Choose one or more of these 10 meanings for the word *wise* that you think ties into this testimony.

[ ] wise   [ ] strategic
[ ] cunning   [ ] crafty
[ ] intelligent   [ ] skillful
[ ] artful   [ ] subtle
[ ] learned   [ ] shrewd

Validation

Experience God's power as you read this book! I was there for the story you just read and many other times. This book will challenge Christians everywhere to get out of the cookie cutter mold! Get ready for the ride of your life. This book is a must read!

William Henderson III
Bill's son

CHAPTER 11

Barmaid to Handmaiden

"But whosoever drinketh of the water that I shall give him shall never thirst; but the water that I shall give him shall be in him a well of water springing up into everlasting life." (John 4:14 KJV)

One Halloween evening I just happened to be dressed up like my favorite personality—Jesus! I was helping lead a team of people in bar evangelism. We targeted a bar located in San Bernardino, California. It happened to be the very place I used to fight and sell drugs before I was born again. That night the bar was sponsoring a Halloween costume contest that I decided to enter. It was a perfect opportunity to invade the bar to share Jesus in a cunning way.

There were many other contestants besides myself. There were devils, witches, angels, and even a pregnant nun. To my great surprise, they told me that I had won the contest. When I went up front dressed like Jesus to receive my first place cash prize, I asked the master of ceremonies to please hand me the microphone because I needed to preach to my congregation. He was really laughing at me because he was probably thinking that I was really way out there and this ought to be cute. Little did he know that the Holy Spirit was orchestrating the whole contest.

After I was handed the microphone, I began to preach Jesus and how to be saved. When it dawned on the emcee that I was really preaching the gospel, he did his best to take the microphone out of my hand but I pressed on and didn't allow it until I had a chance to say what the Holy Spirit had put on my heart.

I pulled off my wig and beard so that people could see who I was. Many recognized me as the old Bill Henderson. I knew some of them could not believe what they were seeing and hearing. I said, "You guys know who I am. You know I'm not Jesus. The last time you saw me in this bar, I was a druggie and a brawler, but recently my whole life has been changed because I have accepted Jesus Christ as my Savior." I pointed to an empty booth over against the far wall of the bar and said, "If you want to know more, please come over and talk with me."

I went over, sat down at the booth, opened up my Bible and began reading and praying, "Lord, send me someone."

Before I knew it, one of the barmaids came up and sat next to me. She asked, "You really weren't preaching just now, were you? You are really just in here having fun, aren't you?"

I responded, "You're right, I am having fun. In fact, I am having the time of my life."

She said, "I thought so. For a minute you almost sounded like a real preacher."

I said, "Really? How would you like to do some lines with me?"

"Now you're talking," she said excitedly, thinking I was going to pull out some cocaine.

"Is anybody watching us?" I asked her.

She replied, "No."

So I opened up my Bible to Romans 10:13 as I grabbed a straw off the table. I put the straw into my Bible and up my nose and then I inhaled deeply as if I were snorting cocaine. Religious people would never do anything like this, but he that is wise, wins souls. To reach this world for Jesus, we must take the gospel to their level. I told her, "Wow! What a line!" as I put my finger on the lines in God's Word that I had just sniffed. I began to read to her out loud ...

> "Whoever calls upon the Name of the Lord shall be saved." (Romans 10:13)

Then while putting the straw to my nose, we did some other lines such as, "If you confess with your mouth that Jesus Christ is Lord, and if you believe in your heart that God raised Jesus Christ from the dead, you shall be saved. For with the mouth man confesses unto salvation, and with the heart man believes unto righteousness." Then I said to her, "Here is another line. Jesus Himself said in John 14:6 (KJV), 'I am the Way, the Truth and the Life; no man comes to the Father except by Me.' "

As I continued to do these lines with her, she was so shocked and convicted that she got up from the table and ran into the bathroom. Later, she reluctantly came back and sat down next to me. She said, "When you started snorting the lines of the Bible, I really got angry because moments before we sat down, I was in the bathroom sniffing drugs through a straw. Tell me, how did you know what I was doing?"

"I didn't know what you were doing," I replied, "but obviously God knew because he knows all things about every one of us."

She said, "Are you trying to tell me that God made you sniff the Bible like that?"

I replied, "Well, did God get your attention or not?"

"I guess so," she confessed. She told me that when she was a little girl, she had asked Jesus into her heart. Now after all the bad things she had done over the years, she didn't think that the Lord was with her any more. So then I prayed with her to surrender fully to Jesus and she left that bar for good.

Since then, she no longer is a barmaid but a handmaiden for the Lord. She met a Christian man, got married, and is now serving God and attending church regularly. What a happy ending! How powerful a few lines can be!

Summary

This story reminds us of the Samaritan woman that Jesus talked to at the well. She was at the well to draw water but Jesus was there to give her living water. This barmaid was at the bar (well) to do lines of dope, but the Holy Spirit was there to give her lines of hope.

> "But whosoever drinketh of the water that I shall give him shall never thirst; but the water that I shall give him shall be in him a well of water springing up into everlasting life." (John 4:14 KJV)

The Word of God tells us, "...he that winneth souls is wise" (Proverbs 11:30 KJV). The Hebrew word for *wise* is *chakam*, meaning wise, strategic, cunning, crafty, intelligent, skillful, artful, subtle, learned and shrewd.

Choose one or more of these 10 meanings for the word *wise* that you think ties into this testimony.

[ ] wise   [ ] strategic
[ ] cunning   [ ] crafty
[ ] intelligent   [ ] skillful
[ ] artful   [ ] subtle
[ ] learned   [ ] shrewd

Validation

I've known Bill Henderson for over 25 years and have been there personally for many of the testimonies you are reading. Bill is an example of one whom, through the grace of God, turned his living a radical life for the devil around into radically serving the Lord! I was there when he dressed up like Jesus and preached in the bar on Halloween.

Bill brings to life the reality of the scripture, "Those who know their God will be strong and do exploits in His name." (Daniel 11:32)

Diane Geyer
Ordained Minister and
former Assistant Dean of Women,
Christ for the Nations Institute
Dallas, Texas

CHAPTER 12

Back to Egypt

"And they said, Believe on the Lord
Jesus Christ, and thou shalt be saved,
and thy house." (Acts 16:31 KJV)

Two years after I was saved, my brother
Jim and I had a great burden to reach our
family with the gospel. So we went to Oklahoma City to visit my uncle Allen, his wife
Kelley, other family members and some of
their friends. My uncle Allen and I used to
hang out together when we were in our late
teens and early twenties. He happens to be
one year younger than me because my grandmother had a baby late in life. Jim and I
wanted to tell all of our family members what
Jesus had done for us. When we arrived in
the city, my uncle Allen had just gotten out of
jail for possession of marijuana and a stolen
credit card. He was facing 2 to 5 years in jail
and perhaps more.

We drove by Uncle Allen's house but no one
was home. We had heard that the Oklahoma
State Fair would start at the same time we
were visiting, so we decided to go there to see
if we could spot any of our relatives who
might be working there. The fair was held at
the same time every year and before I was
born again, I used to sell drugs, bootleg whis-
key and bodyguard for a turquoise jeweler

there. Uncle Allen was the first person we ran into. He had been drinking all day and night.

I played a joke on him after I spotted him and his wife leaving the fair that night. My brother and I were wearing big hats that hid our faces. I approached my uncle Allen and handed him a gospel tract printed by Dr. Billy Graham. In a disguised voice, I said, "Jesus loves you and has a plan for your life." He didn't recognize me as we walked away.

Jim and I watched Uncle Allen for the next few minutes. When he got to his car, it wouldn't start. He lifted up the hood and attempted to start the car while at the same time trying to read the gospel tract. I told my brother Jim, "Let's have some more fun with him. Let's run at him like we are going to tackle him." Both of us ran at him but stopped just inches away, smiled, and shook his hand. For a few minutes he was stunned, but happy to see us.

Got Religion?

His first words were, "Tell me if it is true what I heard about you. Did you guys get religion? Are you really going to church and preaching on the streets? Are you really changed and happy? If it's true, I need some of what you got. I am going to warn you, though, that I'm drunk and I'm higher than a Georgia pine."

He told us that he was very scared. He said that while he was in jail, he had grasped the bars and prayed, "God, if you will just get me out of here, I will never smoke pot again."

We ignored the fact that he was drunk and prayed for him right then. We led him in a prayer to accept Jesus as his Savior. I immediately felt a change. He asked us to follow him home and talk more about what had just happened to him.

After arriving at his house, he was shocked to realize that the prayer to receive Jesus also sobered him up. He told his wife Kelley, "I am stone cold sober. I am straight, man." We went inside and I continued to share the gospel with him. Because we had been praying for them for two years, we talked to them about the power of intercessory prayer. We also felt the need to drive from California to talk to them because we did not want them to go to hell. We shared about the miracles and healing that we had seen since we were saved.

Kelley, with great excitement, asked, "Would Jesus heal me?" She told us that she had had a chronic stomach ulcer for years and was in pain even as we spoke.

I said to her, "I believe that Jesus will heal you right now on the spot. When we pray and lay our hands on you, just like the Bible says, you will be healed." Sure enough, we prayed and Jesus healed her instantly. It has been over twenty years and Kelley is still healed.

Going All the Way

Uncle Allen's attention was really focused now because he was worried about an upcoming court date from his prior arrest and wanted prayer for that too. At that point I told him that Jesus would help him only if he would sell out and go all the way. I said, "If there is anything that you need to give up or get out of this house, you need to do it NOW."

After thinking about what I said, Uncle Allen went to his bedroom and brought out two ounces of marijuana. He asked me, "Is this what you mean?" as he showed me the pot. But I really felt that there was even more hidden somewhere in that house.

Again, I told him, "Uncle Allen, if you are holding back anything at all, it will be hard to find favor with the judge or with the Lord." I noticed that his wife Kelley raised her eyebrows and stared at him. He smiled, dropped his head and walked back into the bedroom. This time he came out with a look of relief on his face as he handed me two shoeboxes full of marijuana. There was over two pounds of pot.

I remember that my uncle Allen had shown me a brand new fireplace that he had made because he was a brick mason by trade. I said, "Let's build the first fire in your new fireplace by burning the devil's pot." We made a big fire that night, one that we will never forget. We made sure that the flue was open and prayed that the smoke would not go into the house. The Lord honored our prayer. It was incredible. Needless to say, that night we had church in front of that fireplace.

Over the next few days, we took Uncle Allen with us to the Oklahoma State Fair as we led several more of our relatives and friends to Jesus. During our stay at the fair, we were able to lead another uncle of mine, Ronnie, his wife Liz and their son Bobby to the Lord. They all received the baptism in the Holy Spirit too.

Jim and I decided to go to New Orleans where our dad and other relatives lived. As we were leaving Oklahoma City, I gave Uncle Allen my personal copy of the book entitled *Prayers that Avail Much.* I wrote to him in the book, "Uncle Allen, please pray these prayers daily and watch your life change right before your eyes."

Uncle Allen did continue to pray daily, found incredible favor with the judge and received a deferred sentence and never spent another day behind bars. Uncle Allen also said that his craving for drugs, alcohol and the party life left him the day he was saved. It has been nearly thirty years that Uncle Allen and his family have faithfully served the Lord and continued to attend church. He was also able to lead both his mother and father to the Lord before they died. They had formerly been members of a cult church called The Church of Christian Science. Uncle Allen also led the pastor of that church to the Lord.

After we arrived in Louisiana and over the next few weeks, we led our father Bill Sr. to the Lord, along with our uncle Bobby and his family. Many others were saved during this three-month journey of reaching our family with the gospel of Jesus Christ.

Summary

> "And they said, Believe on the Lord Jesus Christ, and thou shalt be saved, and thy house." (Acts 16:31 KJV)

Never give up on your relatives! As you intercede for them, the Spirit of God will continue to convict them. Even if you are not the one that gets a chance to lead them to Jesus, as you pray, God will be faithful to send a laborer to reap the harvest.

GOD SENDS LABORERS

> "Pray ye therefore the Lord of the harvest, that he will send forth laborers into his harvest." (Matthew 9:38 KJV)

FERVENT PRAYER MAKES A WAY

> "Confess your faults one to another, and pray for one another, that ye may

be healed. The effectual fervent prayer of a righteous man availeth much." (James 5:16 KJV)

The Word of God tells us, "...he that winneth souls is wise" (Proverbs 11:30 KJV). The Hebrew word for wise is *chakam*, meaning wise, strategic, cunning, crafty, intelligent, skillful, artful, subtle, learned and shrewd.

Choose one or more of these 10 meanings for the word *wise* that you think ties into this testimony.

[ ] wise   [ ] strategic
[ ] cunning   [ ] crafty
[ ] intelligent   [ ] skillful
[ ] artful   [ ] subtle
[ ] learned   [ ] shrewd

Validations

Not only is Bill my brother in Christ, but more intimately, my blood brother. I have had both the merited opportunity and the frightful adventure to walk with him through some of the events included in this book, *God's Radical Remnant.*

God put each of us in this world to make a difference and I believe that He has allowed Bill to walk such paths, to face battles documented in the pages of this book, because He could trust him with the victories.

I not only applaud him with my hands, but also with my heart ... for I have returned to the times where, for me, some of life's mysteries were unveiled ... and I have once again reminisced with the *Remnant.*

Jim Henderson
Bill's brother

~~~

Hello Dear Readers,

The story you have just read in the 12th chapter of Brother Bill's book is true. Bill's dedication to bringing the Word of God, salvation and healing to his family was a life-changing miracle for us. Enjoy!

Allen and Kelley Easter
(Bill's uncle and aunt)

ABOUT THE AUTHOR

My Testimony

My purpose in writing this book is to give God all the glory that is due him through any praise or applause I have received from men for the wonderful results these stories will reveal.

When I was 4 years old, I was diagnosed with a crippling disease call "Legg Perthes." My precious mother was told by the doctors that this disease would spread to my whole body and cause the joints and sockets in my body to deteriorate. I was placed in the Queen of Angels Hospital in Los Angeles, California, for 11 months. Today that hospital is called the Dream Center, founded by Pastors Tommy and Matthew Barnett.

After unsuccessful treatment, I was sent home with a leg brace, crutches, and a 2" sole on a special shoe. My mother had faith that somehow God would heal me some day and she would return to that hospital and give God the glory.

One night my mother and I were watching Oral Roberts do a television broadcast from an old-fashioned camp meeting tent. Brother Roberts told the television viewers to put their hands on the television as a point of contact and believe in God for a healing. My mother further reiterated this step of faith by telling me to thank Jesus for my healing until it manifested.

Six weeks passed and one morning when I woke up, my mother cried out for joy, pointing her finger at my leg and saying, "Look son, Jesus grew your leg back like the other one!" You see my right leg was no longer two inches shorter than my left leg.

She took me back to the doctors. They x-rayed me again and told my mother my hip socket that was fifty percent disintegrated was now one hundred percent normal. Reluctantly, the doctors acknowledged that there had been a miracle.

I would like to say that I lived my life for the Lord after this incredible healing, but I am ashamed to say I did not.

By the age of 27 I had rebelled and gotten involved in bouncing bars, street fighting, motorcycle racing and drug dealing. It was through a drug overdose that I cried out to Jesus and totally gave my heart and life to Him. My mother's prayers had not been in vain. Before she died of cancer I promised her that I would see her "when the roll is called up yonder."

My dear sister Carolyn and her husband Bob prayed also and fasted that my two brothers and I would get saved. My sister fasted sugar and told the Lord that she would not touch sugar until I was saved. Within that same year, God honored and answered her prayers.

Throughout the years, I have learned the importance of living in intimacy with the Lord. From the very beginning of my walk with Him, the Word of God has been my guidance and hope. The outflow of the walk of the Spirit is evangelism. Automatically and willingly! That is why I receive no credit for what you read in this book. It is simple and it is for everyone.

Though I have a Doctorate of Divinity gracing the wall of my office, my greatest achievement is the Lord's pleasure and presence in my life.

To receive God's presence, power and provision, takes TIME—times of intimacy with God. This time spent brings about holiness, purity and change. It's worth it! So don't let the Dream Thief steal that time!

Currently my wife Mary Ann and I are blowing a trumpet call for the church to return to her first love. This return is the ONLY way a unity of Spirit and purpose among believers can result in true repentance and a renewed commitment to fulfill the Great Commission through RADICAL EVAN-GELISM!

This ministry has resulted in revival in many churches and reports of miracles still abound. We are committed to conducting revival services and seminars for soul-winning, providing international disaster relief and assisting in food and clothing distribution to the needy as strategic acts of mercy in an effort to reach the lost.

As an apostolic evangelistic team with a prophetic edge, we travel the world imparting God's power and training God's people while there is still time.

My sincerest love and gratitude to all who embrace the truths in this book and follow the RADICAL within their hearts.

Bill Henderson

Endorsements

~~~

God's Radical Remnant is filled with exciting proof of God's heart for those who don't know Him. The stories are incredible. You'll be amazed as you read of God's love and power, and know beyond question that He can use you to win people to Him. This is an awesome book!

Dutch Sheets
Pastor and Author

~~~

I personally know Bill and his heart for street ministry and the faithless. He is one of a handful who is actually going where few are willing to go. Bill and Mary Ann have gladly dedicated their lives to reaching the outcasts of our society.

Nicky Cruz
Nicky Cruz Outreach Ministries

~~~

Within the pages of this book is the very heartbeat of God. SOULS! These encounters are the result of not only the faith and obedience of Bill Henderson, but also of a growing revelation and mounting movement of the Apostolic and Prophetic restoration within the church today.

This book is for believers of all denominational backgrounds. Read it and prepare to receive a new impartation of God's heartbeat for the lost.

Dr. T. L. Lowery
T. L. Lowery Global Foundation

~~~

Bill Henderson is a radical man of God and a real street witness. He is a threat to the devil's domain wherever he goes. Although anchored in the Word of God, this book applies the message of Jesus to the world where the people are God's Radical Remnant. This book is exciting, informative, inspiring, empowering and true!

I've been with Bill from New York to Hollywood to Rio and he is radical and strong, but tender in compassion and love in the likeness of the Lord Jesus. Bill is a real street sweeper for Jesus! Go! Go! Go!

Arthur Blessitt
International Evangelist and Author

~~~

Bill is a true man of God with a heart for evangelism like few I have ever known. His boldness is from a commitment to follow Jesus whatever the cost. I have known Bill for over twenty-five years and have witnessed his consistency and obedience in the face of trials and opposition. This book is a must read!

Steve Brock
Evangelist/Singer

~~~

One of the most exciting things for any believer is to experience the mighty power of the gospel of Jesus Christ in demonstration. More than anything else, our purpose in life is to know Jesus and make him known. Bill Henderson not only writes about soul winning, he also lives it. The powerful stories in this book will capture your imagination and build faith as you see the Holy Spirit use ordinary people to do extraordinary things.

I am fascinated by the testimonies in this book. What begins as a normal everyday activity somehow, by the working of the Holy Spirit, becomes a supernatural platform to reach even the hardest of sinners. This book will challenge you to be a soul winner, build your faith for demonstration and make Jesus real! *God's Radical Remnant* proves that anybody who loves Jesus can be a soul winner. Are you one of the remnants?

Your partner,
Jonas Clark
Spirit of Life Ministries
Hallandale, Florida

~~~

I met Bill in 1988. When I went to Jerusalem with him, I saw the character of God in Bill. I have been encouraged by his walk in the Lord. I watched him on TBN and saw a man of God with a desire to see the lost saved.

Bill has an enthusiasm for Jesus Christ that is unparalleled. I have been with him when miracles manifested through his preaching. He has a real compassion for drug addicts, gangs and young people as well as anyone who will listen to his words of love, comfort and hope.

The truths in this book will live on long after other books are read. I am honored and happy to lend my endorsement to this wonderful, timely book called *God's Radical Remnant!*

Mary K. Baxter
Author of *Divine Revelation of Hell*

~~~

My friend Bill Henderson is an unstoppable force for evangelizing the world today. I've known Bill for almost 20 years and he has remained consistent in his unswerving desire to serve Jesus by sharing the Good News that changed his life. He is unashamed of the Gospel and unafraid to boldly proclaim the message of Jesus to anyone he meets. At the same time, Bill knows how to be sensitive to the lost and how to be led by the Spirit in every witnessing situation.

You will do yourself a great service by reading and learning and doing what this book teaches. Then one day you will stand before our Lord and hear what will surely be said to Bill Henderson... "Well done, good and faithful servant."

Jerry Davis, Founder
Christian World Embassy/
Good News In Bad News Places

~~~

"And what does the Lord require of you but to do justice, to love mercy and to walk humbly with your God."

This describes Brother Bill. I have known Bill and Mary Ann Henderson for several years now and have enjoyed great moments of praying with them for God's blessing on their lives and ministry. Bill and Mary Ann are both anointed vessels of our Lord.

In this book, Brother Bill has put together a lot of interesting, real life, radical evangelism experiences. They prove that God does open doors that no man can shut as we too accept challenges to become a participator in that Radical Remnant whom God has anointed to help bring in the end-time harvest of souls. I believe this book will be a blessing and a challenge to the body of Christ to win the lost at any cost.

Thank you, Brother Bill, for allowing me to be a part of this blessed adventure.

Dr Larry Tedder
D. Min. Ph. D

~~~

What an inspiration and honor it is to know Bill Henderson, and more importantly, experience the love of God that flows through his life. This book will not only challenge your faith, but it will also put a demand on every believer to leave their comfort zone and become radical and abandoned to the only real reason for living—Jesus Christ!

These encounters are real and carry the same anointing that we read of in the second chapter of Acts.

Take time to absorb and spiritually digest this book for I believe it represents the very heart of God—to go and reach those who are outside the four walls of the church and compel them to come into the Kingdom of God while there is still time.

Thank you, Bill, for your boldness and love for God.

Dr. Lonnie Stewart
Founder, International Spirit of Truth

~~~

I have known Bill Henderson for 27 years. He credits me with being a Father in the Lord to him. But as Paul wrote, I say like Paul "Unto me

who is least of all saints is this grace given"—
that Bill and I should preach among the gentiles
the priceless riches of CHRIST. When we see THE
LORD we want to hear, "Well done thou good and
faithful servant. Enter into the joy of THE LORD".

All these years I have known Bill, I have witnessed his faithfulness and he has run the race
in spite of adversity. I have a love for him as if he
were my son.

You'll enjoy this book!
Max Rapoport

~~~

Rescue ministry is a truly amazing environ-
ment. Miracles are happening every day. Having
served the part of our community that most do
not see in their local church, it gives me great
pleasure to be able to support Bill Henderson
and his first book.

The rescue mission experiences revival each
time Bill comes and shares his love for God with
the people our ministry assists. We are unashamed to open up our outreach to a man who
is on fire for the Lord. The guests at the Mission
relate to these testimonies. Radical Christianity
requires fire and many come to watch Bill burn.

This ministry is blessed by Bill's defense of the
poorest. (Matthew 25)

Reaching out to the least for the King,
Rev. Joseph Vazquez
Executive Director, Springs Rescue Mission
Colorado Spring, Colorado

~~~

Having worked with Bill on the streets for a number years, I have witnessed the calling, anointing and boldness operate through him like I have never seen in another. This book is a compilation of what the hand of God can do through a committed vessel—testimony to the power of God at work today outside the four walls of the church.

Ron Radachy
Co-director, Oasis of Hollywood

~~~

Bill's book will grab you by the heart and fill you with the unction of compassion. His accounts of true cutting-edge evangelistic action will stir you to new acts of boldness in your own life. I have known Bill for 25 of my 35 years as a soul winner and street preacher. He is a true evangelist with the gifts of teaching and equipping others.

Scott Crawford
Evangelist

~~~

I've ministered with Bill and Mary Ann in many prophetic meetings. As a prophetic minister of God, the impartation I have received from Bill's gift of evangelism has increased my anointing to a whole new level.

Bill is a key in this apostolic hour for reformation of apostles and prophets. Bill carries the new wine with a whole new call for worldwide prophetic evangelism. His quick wit and piercing truths will move you in this book. His love and compassion for the lost are as real as Jesus' love. He always cares for the poor, the fatherless and the widow. This book will give you a whole new wineskin.

Shirley Strand
Wind of the Spirit Ministries

~~~

As Bill's pastor for 12 years, I can personally vouch for this man of God's character and calling. The night of Bill's 6-year old daughter Jessica's death will never be forgotten by me or the many others who saw how Bill's love for lost people and vengeance toward the enemy motivated him to win, in those very early morning hours on the hospital grounds, eight people to the Lord.

Bill is always and at all times the consummate soul winner. His passion is reaching lost souls with the good news of Jesus Christ. He is truly a "Son of Thunder." Not only have I been personally challenged to win souls for Christ, but my congregation, under Bill's ministry, has been highly motivated, stirred, challenged and equipped to go forth and fulfill the Great Commission.

I highly recommend this book to every person who desires to go forth and bear eternal fruit for the Master.

Pastor Matt Stoehr
The River at West Coast Christian Center

~~~

BILL HENDERSON IS A RADICAL, as defined in the American Heritage Dictionary of the English Language; *"departing markedly from the usual; extreme."*

BILL HENDERSON IS A RADICAL. American Heritage also defines radical as *"One who advocates revolutionary change."* Bill advocates revolutionary change in the unbeliever.

He advocates a one-step program; come to Jesus and be radically changed by His Holy Ghost. Unashamed of the Gospel, this is the message Bill boldly preaches.

BILL HENDERSON IS A RADICAL. Radical in slang is defined as *"excellent, wonderful."* Bill is both of these. He is an excellent brother in the Lord.

He preaches the life-changing Gospel message with boldness and conviction, all the while with tears in his eyes and a broken heart for the lost who are perishing.

Bill is a friend to sinners, a Holy Ghost preacher, and is powerfully anointed for this urgent hour.

Bill has been baptized by fire and hand-picked by God to spearhead *"God's Radical Remnant."*

Bobby Chance
Director, Streetwise Ministry

~~~

I have worked with Bill Henderson many times over the last eighteen years, both on the streets and in the prisons. He has proven himself to be a man of God who operates with the fervor of the spirit of John the Baptist for evangelism. I have seen him operate in his giftings as an end-time prophetic evangelist, always with compassion for the lost and hurting.

I count it a privilege to have Bill as both a friend and a partner in evangelism.

Glenda Rambo
Revealing God's Glory Ministries

~ ~ ~

The heart of this book, God's Radical Remnant, will give you a glimpse into the life of Bill Henderson. Not only will you read true life stories of reaching others with the Good News, but you will see how you, with the Holy Spirit's help, can do the very same thing too.

Scott Hinkle
Evangelist and Author
Phoenix, Arizona

~ ~ ~

Bill Henderson's passion to win souls and to see an army of soul winners raised up in these days comes through so loud and clear.

Bill's personal experiences along with his understanding of the scriptures will motivate each of us to become more radical in our approach to the end-time harvest.

Billy Burke
Billy Burke Ministries

~~~

Some of my most radical experiences in evangelism have been with Bill Henderson. I've known Bill for over twenty years. I pray as you read this book, a seed will be birthed in you that will take you on a radical journey in God's purpose for your life; reaching many other lives for the kingdom of God.

Mark Johnson
Forerunner Ministries
Minneapolis, Minnesota

~~~

Bill Henderson is a God-called, Holy Spirit-anointed frontline warrior of God's grace! I've known him for over 25 years and the fire of God's love in his soul has not dimmed, but only grown brighter and hotter with each passing year!

Proverbs 11:30 (Amplified) reads: "He that is wise captures human lives for God." Bill is not just a soul-winner counting scalps, but a "life-capturer" for our Lord!

The contagious, evangelistic joy and zeal in his heart (& this book) will capture and ignite your heart as well, with a fresh fire ...and the matchless love of our Lord Jesus Christ... Who died so that none might perish... but all might come to repentance and back home to the Father! " You will never regret reading this book ...and getting copies for others to catch the fire as well!"

Jonathan Gainsbrugh
Evangelist/Author of *Take Him To the Streets*

~~~

I have watched Bill Henderson on TBN for many years and recently met him in person for the first time at the Benny Hinn, Oklahoma City Crusade. His boldness for Jesus Christ is remarkable. As I was reading, the anointing was like fire emanating from *God's Radical Remnant.*

All those who read this book will see how profitable it is to be led by the Holy Spirit and be willing and obedient to all He tells you to do as His occasion serves. 1 Samuel 10: 6 and 7 states, "And the Spirit of the Lord will come upon thee, and thou shalt prophesy with them, and shalt be turned into another man. And let it be, when these signs are come unto thee, that thou do as occasion serve thee; for God is with thee."

Dr. Anthony L. Bright
PhD, D.D. D.R.E., PhD, ThD, D.Min, PhD
Founder and President,
Worldnet Christ Ministries
St. Louis, Missouri

~~~

To read complete endorsements and what others have to say about Bill Henderson and his radical evangelism, please visit the Henderson International Ministries Web site
<u>www.word-onthestreet.com</u>

Meet Jesus

We would like to take this opportunity to introduce you to the Lord Jesus Christ! To accept Him as your personal Lord and Savior, follow these steps:

A   Acknowledge that you are a sinner in need of a Savior.
Romans 3:23 says, "For all have sinned and fall short of the glory of God." (NKJV)

B   Believe that God sent Jesus as the only way to heaven and forgiveness of sins.
Romans 10:9 says, "Believe in your heart that God raised Him from the dead and you will be saved." (NKJV)

C   Confess with your mouth—tell others openly of your commitment to Jesus.
Romans 10:10 says, "For with the heart one believes to righteousness, and with the mouth confession is made to salvation." (NKJV)

If you want to enter the kingdom of heaven, pray this prayer:

Lord, I am a sinner and I am in need of a savior to cleanse me from my sins. I believe that Jesus Christ is the only one who can do that. I ask you to forgive me of my sins and come into my heart and be the Lord of my life. Satan, you have no more authority in my life. From this day forward I confess Jesus Christ as my personal Lord and Savior. Thank you Lord Jesus for saving my soul. In Jesus' name I pray. Amen.

If you prayed that prayer out of a sincere heart before God, you can rejoice because you are now a born again child of God and you have escaped the flames of hell!

Baptism is essential to the Christian walk, and so is finding a good church that preaches the Word of God without compromise, and one that exhibits the love of Christ. Ask the Lord to lead you to the right church. If we can be of any support or help, please do not hesitate to contact us.

God has a purpose for your life and you can discover that purpose by finding your place in the Kingdom of God through earnestly seeking the Lord's will for your life. Matthew 6:33 says, "But seek first the kingdom of God and His righteousness, and all these things shall be added to you." (NKJV)

We would be truly blessed to know of your decision to follow Jesus. Please e-mail or write if you are able. God bless you and welcome to the body of Christ!

E-mail   www.word-onthestreet.com

Or mail a note to:
    Henderson International Ministries
    4164 Austin Bluffs Parkway #359
    Colorado Springs, CO 80918